HUNZA LAND

*The Fabulous Health
and Youth Wonderland
of the World*

By
DR. ALLEN E. BANIK

and
RENÉE TAYLOR

1958

WHITEHORN PUBLISHING COMPANY
Long Beach   California

DEDICATION

This book is dedicated to my friend, Art Linkletter, in grateful appreciation for his generous support and sponsorship of my trip to Hunza. He has been instrumental in inspiring me to share with you the message of a better way of living through a balance of the physical, mental and spiritual aspects of man.

TABLE OF CONTENTS

Introduction, *by Art Linkletter*		11
Preface		13

Chapter

1.	Journey to a Hidden Land	21
2.	The Road to Hunza	59
3.	Introduction to Hunza	93
4.	Hunza Farming and Food	117
5.	Hunza Families and Hunza Health	135
6.	Farewell to Hunza	149
7.	The Hunza Lesson	173
8.	The Inspiration of Hunza	209
	Appendix: Questions and Answers	221

LIST OF ILLUSTRATIONS

These illustrations will be found between pages 96 and 97:

    Art Linkletter and the author
    The "printing press" of *Hilal,* a Pakistan Government newspaper
    A Pakistan cloth factory
    A Pakistan bazaar
    A snack bar outside a bazaar
    A *tanga*
    Dangerous flight
    Six men and a jeep
    The author and a Hunza guide
    Mt. Rakaposhi
    The author and the Mir's uncle

These illustrations will be found between pages 192 and 193:

    The Mir's palace
    The Mir, his sons and the author
    A Hunza child
    Hunza Land terraces
    The author before the Mir's Council of Elders
    Hunza women
    The author and a group of Hunzakuts after an eye examination
    The author examining a Hunza Water gourd

INTRODUCTION

I HAVE always claimed that there is no stunt too impossible for us to suggest on the PEOPLE ARE FUNNY show. There are volunteers for whatever wild or zany gag we can dream up. I have seen a studio full of women blithely agree to step into a cage with a savage lion. I have seen hands go up all over an audience when I've asked for someone to make his first parachute jump out of an airplane over Beverly Hills. And I was not surprised to find volunteers by the score for a rocket trip to the moon.

But the trip to Hunza required a very special kind of volunteer. We could easily have asked for someone at random in our studio audience—but for an examination of the strange people in the faraway Himalayas, we needed a man with a scientific background and a deep interest in the study of geriatrics.

Dr. Banik proved to be that man, an optometrist living in Kearney, Nebraska, whose name came up repeatedly in our quest for a hobbyist who pursued the provocative study of old age.

We flew a PEOPLE ARE FUNNY scout to his home town to interview him, to make sure he was the right man for this kind of stunt. The report came back: "great." Dr. Banik was the ideal guest: enthusiastic, cooperative, curious, happy—and an intelligent observer.

He, and Hunza, made one of the most successful episodes in our show's history. My only regret was that time-on-the-air did not permit the full story of his eventful trip to be told. Happily, this book fills in the fascinating details and unfolds the complete story of one of the most unusual postage-stamp countries in the world. The people and their curious customs, as well as their amazing health record, form the background for a saga that rivals Marco Polo's adventures.

ART LINKLETTER

PREFACE

IN THE following pages I have endeavored to bring the reader information acquired in a visit to Hunza. The trip was sponsored and made possible through Art Linkletter and the *People Are Funny* Productions.*

Hunza is a unique little country in the Himalaya valley isolated until recently from contact with the outside world. Many reasons stimulated my desire to learn more about these amazing people through personal observation. It began in 1937 when I first read a magazine article describing a virtually unknown people whose vigor and long life (100 to

---

* An NBC Television Network show—once a week, Saturday—originating in Los Angeles, California, with host Art Linkletter.

120 years) defied belief. These are the Hunzukuts, the citizens of Hunza—tiny, autonomous, with a current population of some 25,000, tucked away between mountain peaks rising ten to nineteen thousand feet above their fertile valley only eighteen miles from Soviet Russia where the borders of that country meet China and Pakistan (West). For nearly two thousand years these phenomenal people have lived in almost complete isolation from the rest of the world.

This race, which has survived through centuries, is remarkable for its vigor and virility. They are fair-skinned, and assumed to be Caucasian. Their methods of agriculture and soil preservation have become a legend to the rest of the world. Scientists and doctors fortunate enough to visit the Hunzukuts and study their way of life have attributed the extraordinary health and vigor of the people primarily to their diet and their methods of growing food. Apparently their bodies have thereby become resistant to disease.

I was eager to visit Hunza to learn everything I could about the country, the people, their cus-

PREFACE

toms and living conditions. However, my chances of ever making the trip seemed nil. Being a professional man, I had to depend on my practice for my primary income, and I could hardly afford an expensive journey to such a distant land. My activities were more or less limited to my own state of Nebraska, and I had done very little traveling abroad.

I cannot even begin to express my great appreciation and gratitude to Art Linkletter, personally, and *People Are Funny* Productions for providing me with the opportunity to make my Hunza dream come true. Art's understanding and generosity in financing the trip not only fulfilled my dream but contributed to changing my whole life.

My sincere thanks go to the Mir and Rani of Hunza, beloved rulers of the world's healthiest people, for their warm welcome and kind hospitality during my stay in their country, as well as for their assistance in making my research possible.

I am also deeply indebted to Mr. Ted Kennedy, telecast announcer for KHAS-TV, Hastings,

Nebraska, who kept the people of central Nebraska informed of my movements at all times; and to Mr. Henry Mann, of E. Leitz, Inc., for presenting me with two beautiful Leica M3 cameras, which made it possible for me to take the many pictures I am sharing with people of my country through this book and through the showing of slides at lectures. Neither can I neglect to mention my wife Elane and daughter Nola for standing by so lovingly and patiently during the long period of waiting and then through the uncertainty of the actual trip.

This book could never have been written without the wise counsel and tireless efforts of Renée Taylor. I am most grateful to Ruth Boyd for hours and hours of typing and re-typing, and to Lee Shaw for his help in arranging the research material.

Since my return, I have clarified all my thoughts in a definite pattern. This trip widened my horizons geographically and mentally. What used to be a vague picture has now crystallized into a message which I hope to bring to the attention of everyone through lectures and printed material.

PREFACE

This book has been written to help you understand the relation of soil to your health and diet, and subsequently the health of our nation. As you plan the future of your children don't overlook the science of nutrition and the physical body. Learn the facts; become aware of the truth and build a strong, healthy America.

We do not live alone, neither do we work alone. Only by the combined efforts to a common cause can we move the mountains before us, and I humbly submit my small contribution to you. I hope it will grow in your heart as it did in mine.

ALLEN E. BANIK

HUNZA LAND

CHAPTER ONE

JOURNEY TO A HIDDEN LAND

SETTLING back in the comfortable lounge chair of an American Airlines plane headed *west* seems a strange way to begin fulfillment of a twenty years' dream. My goal lay 12,000 miles *east* in the craggy vastness of the Himalayas. A dream can be made to seem logical; the means of fulfillment always seem miraculous.

As the plane flew west toward California on that April day in 1958, I reflected on how the "miracle" had happened. One afternoon I answered my phone expecting a routine call, but the operator informed me that Hollywood was calling. This was a real surprise as I knew no one in that

HUNZA LAND

part of California. The first thought to cross my mind was: "Now which one of my relatives has run out of money?"

In a moment or two a cordial voice came over the wire: "Dr. Banik, this is Irving Atkins. I represent *People Are Funny* Productions here in Hollywood. Art Linkletter received a letter from you about eight months ago in which you described the mysterious land of Hunza. In your letter you suggested we send someone to Hunza and we have chosen *you* to go! Would you be willing to make a rugged trip like that?"

I was bewildered by Mr. Atkins' words. A letter to Art Linkletter? When did I write it? But of course. Some time ago while watching the show on TV, I had a sudden impulse to write Mr. Linkletter about Hunza land and its wonderful people. At the end of the program I did just that, and sent the letter off the next morning, suggesting that Art Linkletter send someone to Hunza to bring back facts about the people's health, longevity and way of life. But the chance of being chosen as the lucky one to go never entered my mind.

I was involved in research in optometry when I came across an article describing the extraordinary people of Hunza. The story was so fascinating that I resolved to learn as much about the subject as I could. I collected articles, news reports, pamphlets and books. *The Wheel of Health,* by Dr. Wrench, first printed in 1938 in England, was one book that I read and re-read. This scholarly tribute to Hunza made a deep and lasting impression on my mind.

Dr. Wrench said: "A good deal is known about the Hunza people, but superficially rather than intimately. They are still a people peculiarly themselves. They have preserved their remoteness from the ways and habits of the modern world, and with it those methods of life which contribute to or cause the excellent physique and bodily health which is theirs."*

I was anxious to compare the visual acuity and the condition of the blood vessels in the Hunzukuts' eyes with those of our citizens. Would the

* Wrench, C. T., *The Wheel of Health.* London: C. W. Daniel Co., Ltd.

HUNZA LAND

robust constitution of the people of Hunza be reflected in better vision and freedom from the weaknesses of eyesight to which we are prone?

Picture, if you can, a place as far away as the mind's eye can reach. Travel with me to a land where six mountain ranges, awe-inspiring in their majesty, converge in that mysterious place where Russia, China and Pakistan meet. Here—just eighteen miles from Russia's southern border—just beyond the northern tip of Pakistan and nestled between rocky ramparts ten to nineteen thousand feet high, lies the Shangri-La of my dreams.

The few arable acres of this tiny country have sustained its meager population for nearly 2,000 years in almost complete isolation from the rest of the world. An ancient trade route from Sinkiang province in China to Gilgit (in what is now Pakistan, West) ran through the towering mountains which encircle the Hunza valley. This hazardous trail, in many places not more than twenty-four inches wide, gave precarious passage to caravans carrying priceless cargoes between China and India.

The fair-skinned people of Hunza trace their lineage to soldiers of Alexander the Great, who took Persian wives and then lost themselves by choice in the valley, a comparatively short distance off the famous trade route. Whatever their ancestry, the men of Hunza have been able to maintain their isolation and today live in health and happiness to the age of 120 years. It is a land where the people enjoy not only purity of body but also mutual trust and integrity. In spite of being so remote and isolated, these people have become practical engineers without mathematics, successful agriculturalists without chemical knowledge, and the healthiest, longest-lived people in the world without medicine.

Sir Robert McCarrison, who made a thorough study of the Hunza people and spent considerable time performing various experiments with their soil and food, made the following statement: "These people [the Hunzukuts] are unsurpassed by any Indian race in perfection of physique. They are long-lived, vigorous in youth and age, capable

HUNZA LAND

of great endurance, and enjoy a remarkable freedom from disease in general."*

Early in my optometric practice, I began a study of the color and mathematical ratio of the retinal arteries and veins. I became convinced that my findings might have a bearing on the determination of the life-span in man: for it is through the eye that we can observe the circulatory system in action. Medical advances have been phenomenal in the past decade, yet many avenues of approach toward further progress are inviting.

We optometrists faithfully dedicate our ministry to God's most gracious gift, sight, which embraces more than fitting glasses. Just as the eyes are part of the body and can influence the body, so can the body influence the eyes. Eight of the twelve important cranial nerves that supply the body with nervous energy are used directly or indirectly by the eyes. Perhaps the eyes of the Hunzukuts contained some answer to their remarkable vigor and long life.

The fact has been verified that the Hunza civil-

---

* McCarrison, Robert, *Nutrition and Health*. London: Faber and Faber, Ltd.

ization dates back more than 2,000 years and that conditions now are relatively the same as they were then. An interesting opinion is advanced by Dr. Wrench when he writes: "We are now able to see with greater clarity and wider observation that the remarkable physique of this people is not causeless or accidental, nor a happy chance of nature, nor due to fresh mountain air, but it has a long history to support it. The inhabitants of Hunza are exceptional agriculturists now, as they must have been in the past, and by their character they have preserved—century after century—a quality of agriculture which has rendered to them through food its return gift of perfect physique and health."* This theory interested me in a study of Hunza and its people as a possible clue to health and longevity. Perhaps the answer lay in the soil and not in the actual food.

My emotions were mixed as the plane's wheels touched down on the International Airport in Los Angeles. Of course I was elated by the thought that

* Wrench, *op. cit.*

my adventure was beginning, but I was somewhat awed by the approaching meeting with the fabulous people of the entertainment world. However, I quickly realized that I should have had no concern on this score. I was welcomed cordially by *People Are Funny* representatives and whisked to beautiful offices, where I met many gracious and efficient members of the staff.

Needless to say, the highlight of my Hollywood visit was meeting Art Linkletter—an experience I shall never forget. His on-stage personality is known to millions, but off-stage he is even more friendly and congenial. His warmth and sincerity are genuine. One of his associates told me that during the fourteen years he had known Art, he had never seen him lose his temper. I can well believe it.

The size of the television studios was impressive and the perfectly co-ordinated confusion was amazing. As I stumbled over power lines, blinked at bright lights, bumped into people, and dodged mobile camera cranes, I tried to concentrate on the simple part I was to do on the show. Thanks to the patience, understanding and master-showmanship of Art, I carried off my bit passably well.

The "stunt" had now become a serious assignment. What had been said on the show had to be carried out. The public would expect to hear the results upon my return from Hunza.

Preliminary steps for my trip were begun immediately. The Linkletter organization swung into action. There were inoculations to take, passport and visas to procure, the itinerary to map, men to be contacted along the route, reservations to make, and equipment and luggage to buy. The magnitude and detail of the plans are suggested by the fact that pre-arrangements had to be made even for such things as jeeps, burros, guides, etc.

It soon became apparent that the entire trip hinged on securing Pakistan and Hunza visas and special permission to enter these countries even after the visas had been obtained. Hunza is located beyond the northern tip of West Pakistan, the government of which controls the foreign relations

HUNZA LAND

program of Hunza. Negotiations for entrance permission were carried out through the Pakistan Embassy in Washington, D. C., and although United States relations with Pakistan are cordial, citizens of our country (and those of all other countries) are closely screened before being allowed to enter. The red tape involved in these negotiations prolonged the delay week after week, from April through June, July, August and September. I had, of course, returned to my practice after the Hollywood sojourn, and occasionally I doubted that our plans would ever be carried out.

During this waiting period I received a long distance call from Mr. Franc Shor of *National Geographic Magazine*. He said he had heard I was going to make the Hunza trip and asked my age. When he heard I was fifty-two there was a silence. Then he said, "Good Heavens, man, you will never make it! I was only thirty-three when I entered Hunza in 1953, and although I was in excellent condition, I just barely made it! I don't want to discourage you, but there are so many things you should know before you attempt such a trip that I feel it my duty to inform you at this time."

He recounted some of the hazards I might look forward to, including a nerve-shattering flight through mountain canyons, narrow ledges to negotiate at dizzy heights, dangerous rock slides, and so on.

Dumfounded, I listened to his description. Is this the road to Hunza? I anticipated a rough trip, but not to that extent. The rest of the day I worried considerably. I could see myself on a high ledge looking down at seeemingly bottomless chasms, with distant rocky crags even farther below, when suddenly a strong gust of wind would sweep me to a mangled death.

Then I recollected my childhood days when I had dared to climb a hundred-foot windmill and dangle my feet from the platform. There, too, a sudden gust of wind could have turned the wheel of the mill and swept me off the platform. I wasn't afraid then . . . why should I be now?

Nevertheless, the following day I phoned Mr.

Atkins in Hollywood and told him the story. He assured me that although he hoped I would make the trip, the decision was entirely up to me. After thinking it over carefully, I decided that I certainly would go to Hunza as I had agreed. My later experiences, however, demonstrated that Mr. Shor's advice was accurate and that he had had my welfare in mind.

Finally, early in October, word came that I was to leave for Washington at once to receive my credentials. In Washington I met Major M. Hya-ud-din, Senior Military Liaison Officer of the Pakistan Embassy, who expressed deep interest in my Hunza trip. As he knew the route well and was personally acquainted with the Mir (ruler) of Hunza, our conversation was most enlightening. I picked up some suggestions from the Major which I was sure would stand me in good stead both in Pakistan and in Hunza.

There was no time to lose because winter was approaching in that region. As soon as all the formalities were completed, I left for New York City to pick up my plane reservations for the remainder of the trip. There I boarded the Dutch Airlines for Karachi, Pakistan.

We were flying high above the clouds. Listless, I looked out the windows. The strain of the last few days was beginning to tell on me. Unaware of what was actually happening, my thoughts were hazy, my emotions mixed. First I was crazily happy, then scared and jittery like a small schoolboy waiting to be punished. I still wondered if I were dreaming, and at the same time I was afraid the dream might end there and then and the last few days spent in Washington turn out to be only a figment of my imagination.

It was hard for me to accept the responsibility of being the emissary of Mr. Linkletter's organization . . . I, a simple country doctor, in the role of a hero! It was too much to bear all at once and so alone. As I sat in the spacious cabin, oblivious to all that was going on around me, my heart was beating fast. "You fool," I said to myself. "Of course it is true! Don't you remember how great was your desire to meet the people of Hunza, to visit their country, to find out how they live and what they think? You always wanted to get first-hand information. Haven't you been dreaming of this for twenty long years? And now when it has actually happened you are afraid!"

The airliner began to descend. Karachi airport was below. Then the engines stopped, and with the last turn of the propellers my confused emotions came to a stop too.

Here I boarded a Pakistan airliner to Rawalpindi in North Pakistan, at the foothills of the Himalayas. On my arrival bad news greeted me. "Five feet of snow in the passes!" Roads were closed, and there would be no entry into Hunza until spring. After a few days' visit in the city, I had no choice but to retrace my route and return to Nebraska. When I phoned Art Linkletter he was sincerely disappointed for me. However, with characteristic generosity, he assured me that next year I would make another trip—this time all the way to Hunza!

It would be months before I could start out again!

JOURNEY TO A HIDDEN LAND

True, I was impatient, but the interval would allow me to recheck my equipment in the light of the actual traveling experience of making this initial attempt to get to Hunza. I realized there were some items which could be added advantageously. Hours, for example, could be spent in becoming more familiar with the cameras, light meters, and other photographic equipment I would use.

Indeed, my curiosity was whetted by the delay because in Karachi I made my first contact with Middle Eastern people. I heard languages that sounded strange to my ears, and saw dress, architecture and customs that were foreign to my experience. Could these impressions foretell anything about the Hunzukuts and their way of life? Or would the Hunza-valley race be something entirely different, as I had come to believe from reading and from conversations with men who had traveled to the fabled little country?

I kept in touch by mail with the people I had met in Pakistan. My story was of interest to them because many of the officials had been close to the Hunza border but had never entered the country.

HUNZA LAND

The valley was a mystery to them, as it was to most of the rest of the world.

The time of departure for my second trip was scheduled for June 2, 1958. The excitement and exhilaration of adventure took over as I swung into action. "It is really happening," I whispered to myself. By now I was ready to accept my assignment without hesitation or fear.

The whole city joined me in my excitement. Kearney's newspaper, *The Hub,* and KHAS, the near-by TV station, gave me a rousing send-off. Their friendly wishes buoyed me up for the entire trip; often in moments of stress and danger my thoughts would return to Kearney and I found renewed courage to continue.

Setting down again at the Karachi airport was, indeed, like coming home because of the experiences I had enjoyed in this Pakistan city on my visit the year before. I looked forward eagerly to meeting the many friends I had made at that time. I knew that even my former bearers (bellhops) would be glad to see me, for friendships can be made readily among any people—no matter how different their status or mode of life—when decency and respect are mutual.

Pakistan was of particular interest to me because all dealings of the Hunzukuts with the outside world necessarily are channeled through Pakistan.

As the prime purpose of my visit to Hunza was to study the health conditions among the population, I was naturally curious to learn about the health aspect of other countries I had visited en route. For example, the teeth of the Pakistanians were a revelation to me. They were smooth, regular, shiny and perfect. I wondered how they preserved their teeth in this amazing fashion. Do they use toothbrushes? Is good diet a factor? Just what do they eat?

Dr. Hassan, a Karachi physician, gave me some interesting information. "Our children," he told me, "are very poor. They do not eat between meals, and there are no carbonated beverages, sweets, pastries or ice cream to tempt them. Instead, they eat whole grains made into *chappati* and bread, which becomes very difficult to chew when hard.

HUNZA LAND

Garden vegetables, milk products, fruits and some meat make up the balance of their diet. As for toothbrushes and toothpaste, they have none. However, they do go to the market and get tiny twigs, which they bite into threads at one end and then use as a brush to rid the teeth of food particles."

I thought of the children in the United States—those who cannot afford limitless soft drinks, ice cream, candy and pastry generally enjoy better health than the "more fortunate." Good health originates inside the body. Do spots in teeth come from within, rather than from without?

We imagine germs suddenly surrounding our teeth, searching for vulnerable spots to attack—as though they gloated in destroying our precious enamel. Then by the simple expedient of fluoridation and magic toothpaste, we hope to banish these germs forever.

Two weeks in the Hotel Metropole offered ample opportunity for good times with new acquaintances from Karachi, Western Europe, and even a few tourists from the United States. The hotel was built in blockhouse shape, its rooms laid out on four sides of a large square patio or garden made beautiful by colored sidewalks, green lawns and foliage, and twinkling lights. Each night a good orchestra played dance tunes for the Karachi elite. The mystery of the Orient made the setting much more exciting than anything similar I had experienced in the States.

One afternoon as I was having cakes and tea with a Spanish lady on the patio, two huge cats jumped up on the vacant chairs and tried to snatch the food. I removed the chairs and was attempting to scatter the cats by waving a folded newspaper when our cakes disappeared with a loud *swish*. A Pakistan hawk, or kite, had flown off with the pastry in his talons! It was my first experience with these birds which are constantly circling above. Needless to say, the lady and I moved under the protection of an awning.

It is the custom of Pakistanian ladies to wear a jewel in the left nostril. The wealthier the lady, the more precious the jewel. My first thought on seeing a jewel worn in this way was that it had slipped, and I was about to warn the lady of the mishap. However, I spied several others adorned in this strange fashion, and learned then of the custom of piercing the nostril in the same way that women's ears are pierced in our country. The idea is rather pleasing when you get accustomed to it.

How different this Karachi interlude was from my customary mode of life in Nebraska! The strange façades of the buildings; the Asian faces of the busy populace; the confusing, milling mass of camel carts, peddlers, bicycles, pushcarts; the hordes of nondescript children—all were strange and fascinating to me.

My schedule called for a seven-hundred-mile jump north to Rawalpindi, the next-to-last stopping point on my trek to Hunza. We took off from the Karachi airport at five in the morning. There were several Americans aboard, mostly oilmen and engineers from Texas, and good conversation made the time pass quickly.

Below stretched vast desert grasslands and occasional large patches of agricultural land. Small villages were spaced at great intervals and roads were few. In contrast to the primitive homes mostly in evidence were a few large, more impressive looking structures which, I was told, were built when England had ruled this territory and their officials had demanded luxury.

An hour's stop at Lahore, a large and busy city, enabled me to take pictures and to observe the inhabitants who were at the airport. Re-entering the plane, we headed for Rawalpindi where I was to headquarter until ready to take the hazardous flight to Gilgit. There I expected to meet the Pakistanian cameraman assigned to go with me to Hunza to take pictures for the *People Are Funny* show.

In Rawalpindi I was also to obtain final official approval of my request to enter Hunza. It was to take me two weeks in this city before final permission was granted, and it literally required the United States Army to get me into Hunza!

Commander Maqbool H. Khan and Major Abnul Hasam, of the Pakistan Interservices Public Relations Department, greeted me at the airport and offered their jeep to transport my equipment to the hotel where accommodations had been reserved for me.

HUNZA LAND

The Flashman Hotel rather resembles our motels. American bath facilities and revolving ceiling fans graced my three-room apartment. Though some units had air-conditioning, I asked for one without this comfort as I wanted to acclimate myself to the torrid heat I knew I would be exposed to in the next few weeks. That day the temperature was 112 degrees—moderate for this season of the year. I had always thought Nebraska temperatures a little on the warm side in summer, but here in Pakistan it was *really* hot.

There was a colony of Americans in Rawalpindi, and many American army officers and engineers regularly dined at the hotel. Finding friendly companions was not difficult. In a strange country with unfamiliar customs it seems that friendly Americans always turn up to banish the homesickness blues. United States citizens can be spotted anywhere by the way they walk and talk, and by the cordial way they approach everyone.

The following morning I took a *tanga,* or horse-drawn cab, to General Headquarters to meet Com-

JOURNEY TO A HIDDEN LAND

mander Maqbool and receive my final papers to enter Hunza. The building was only eight blocks away, but the heat was so intense that walking would have been unbearable. I arrived at nine o'clock, as that was the customary start of the business day at home, but I learned that office hours in Rawalpindi extend from seven until twelve-thirty.

Commander Maqbool came out to meet me and extend a warm welcome. Speaking excellent English, he said, "Please come in, Dr. Banik. Have a cup of tea and refresh yourself while you meet our staff." (During warm spells in Kearney I always enjoyed sitting on the porch with a glass of *iced* tea at my elbow. But here in the Middle East you take *hot* tea or nothing. Finally you get used to it.)

Headquarters closely resembled American army barracks. Each building was surrounded by a high woven fence with barbed wire at the top; roofs overhung to provide porch-like protection. Neat hedges enclosed most offices, and attempts to encourage lawns, rosebushes and trees lent a pleasant effect. Pakistanians are noted for their love of gardens, shrubs and trees.

One building of better construction than the others housed the army newspaper for Urdu, the Hindustani language. There is no type for the Urdu language and, consequently, all news copy is written in longhand. The men who do the writing are chosen because of their ability to duplicate the style of their predecessors; when printed, the papers seem to be written in the same handwriting. As each man on the writing staff keeps his job as long as he is physically able to work, the personnel turnover problem is not acute.

In the Commander's office Major Hasam greeted me and introduced other members of the staff. After a proper interval, I turned the conversation to my Hunza trip in the firm belief that my clearance papers were here at Headquarters in good order. I was shocked to be told that my credentials were *not* here and that permission must be granted by the secret service over which their department had no influence.

"I wish they would accept our suggestions," the Commander said, "but Hunza lies in a restricted area and very few people are allowed to enter. I am most willing to help you get permission, but as I am connected only with the Public Relations Department, all I can do is state my opinions. I can certainly tell them I'm sure you are not a Communist, that you have a purpose in entering Hunza, and that this would be a wonderful public relations program for Pakistan. But the power to grant permission lies in their hands."

"Whom am I to contact, then?"

"Colonel Riaz."

"Why, I met him last fall, and he granted me permission then."

"I'm afraid he didn't, Dr. Banik. As you remember, five feet of snow had fallen in the Hunza passes, making entry impossible. Colonel Riaz evidently believed you would not come back to try again."

When I asked if I might get an appointment with Colonel Riaz I was told he was out of town and would not be back for three days!

At first I was angrily impatient at this added delay, but I told the Commander I could probably use the time to advantage—to locate my cameraman, for example. I was pleasantly surprised when he said, "Your cameraman, Mahmood Hussain, is waiting in the next room!"

He was about thirty-five, rather dark in complexion, and nearly bald. He had a cheery twinkle in his eye and a pleasing personality. Shaking my hand with a firm grasp, he said, "Very happy to meet you." During the ensuing conversation, I learned that Mahmood had owned a prosperous camera repair shop and jewelry store in India, and that he was one of the Moslems who had come to Pakistan seeking religious freedom, although it meant sacrificing much that he had.

His movies and still pictures demonstrated remarkable expertness with both types of camera. Mahmood was obviously a master of the light meter; and the pictures indicated a professional understanding of picture composition. It was good to find such a skilled cameraman and amiable companion.

He accepted this assignment reluctantly, however. The money he would receive was quite an attractive aspect, but he also realized the danger involved in reaching Hunza. Although very few people entered the valley, stories about the strenuous and hazardous trip traveled fast. These stories didn't help to attract visitors. Mahmood was aware of the rough journey facing him and could not help being scared. To control the situation, and avoid losing my cameraman, I had to act self-assured regardless of how I felt.

For the next two days I tried to contact the country's key men in government, in the army and in the secret service. I scanned the list of American residents in search of any source of possible influence. No work could be done in the afternoon, and I found myself rising earlier and earlier, until my bearer was bringing my breakfast tea at four-thirty. In Rawalpindi this kind of schedule is not unusual.

Promptly at seven on the third day, I hailed a *tanga* and taxied to Headquarters.

Commander Maqbool greeted me. "Well, Dr.

Banik, the time has arrived. Today we shall see whether or not you go to Hunza! I will phone Colonel Riaz now."

While he was getting the connection, I suggested he arrange an appointment rather than trust negotiations to a telephone conversation. He nodded agreement, and a ten o'clock meeting was arranged. A sporty little English roadster carried us to the sentry gate where the Commander showed his card and applied for admission. The sentry shook his head, and a heated discussion ensued in a language I could not understand.

I knew something was wrong, as the Commander became quite indignant. His ire was matched by the sentry, who motioned us to wait. Then he disappeared, apparently to consult a higher authority.

While we waited, the Commander gave me the gist of their conversation, explaining that he was unable to take me in unless I left my camera with the sentry. He argued that, since he had permission to take in his own camera, I should be permitted the same courtesy. Although I wanted a photograph of Colonel Riaz for my personal use,

I sacrificed that desire because I realized that gaining admittance was more important. I handed the camera to the sentry when he returned, and we drove along a winding road to Colonel Riaz' office.

We were ushered into a room where several officers examined my credentials. A few moments later, the Colonel entered from an adjoining room. He was young and wore a well-tailored uniform. His welcoming smile revealed perfect, white teeth beneath a close-cropped mustache. After introductions I offered him an American cigarette, which he politely refused in favor of one of his own brand. A bearer entered with the inevitable pot of tea, and we settled in our chairs to take up the matter of our visit.

Commander Maqbool began the conversation in English: "Dr. Banik is here from the United States under the auspices of a large television program sponsored by Mr. Art Linkletter. [I had previously suggested that he not use the *People Are Funny* title as it might easily be misunderstood.] He is very anxious to go to Hunza to make a study of the people, purely from a scientific viewpoint, and to bring back a report by television to the American people. You may remember that Dr. Banik was here last fall at the time the snows started." Colonel Riaz nodded.

The Commander continued: "Dr. Banik has permission from the Pakistan Embassy in Washington, D.C., and from the Prime Minister of Pakistan. Colonel Malik, of Karachi, routed the trip through here. Since this is Dr. Banik's second attempt, made at a cost of thousands of dollars, he is most anxious to complete the assignment."

"Yes, I know," Colonel Riaz replied, shaking the ashes from his cigarette, "but I am afraid that it is impossible. As you know, Commander, our situation up north is very serious. We are on the verge of war any minute. For every permission we grant, we must allow one of their people to come down here. We must limit this exchange to a minimum." He was brief and to the point as he continued. "I can see no possible way for Dr. Banik to enter Hunza. Now, if you will excuse me, I have an important engagement. My orderly will show you to your car."

With that last statement, he left us sitting, looking blankly at one another as the orderly handed us our helmets.

Here, it seemed, was the well-known stone wall. However, Commander Maqbool had told me General Ayub Khan was the final authority in the country. Although it was difficult to get an audience with the General, if I could get organized opinion behind me, the General might be favorably impressed.

Time was running short. The monsoon rains would arrive in three weeks, and I had to enter Hunza and return before the downpours began; otherwise, there would be a six weeks' delay. I began contacting members of the army, secret service and public relations department. I also talked with Rawalpindi doctors. The Dean of the Medical College invited me to speak before the entire group of one hundred forty physicians, and I was very grateful for the opportunity. Only few Pak-

HUNZA LAND

istanians seemed aware that the people of Hunza are unique examples of health and longevity.

Days passed with no success in sight! Then, one evening on my way to the dining room, I fell in step with Mr. and Mrs. Brevaire, a couple whose quarters adjoined mine in the hotel. Although we had only a nodding acquaintance, they invited me to join them for dinner. The Brevaires seemed to know all about my difficulties in reaching Hunza—as did everybody in the hotel. Art Brevaire, I learned, was an outspoken Frenchman, reared in Switzerland, who had become a citizen of the United States. About sixty-five, he would have made a typical Prussian officer.

When I dejectedly observed that my chances of getting into Hunza looked bleak, Art Brevaire barked, "You are just not seeing the right people!"

"Do you know Colonel Riaz?"

"Sure, I know him, but you've got to see General Ayub Khan. He's your man."

"That's what I'm trying to do!" I cried, almost rising to my feet.

"Now take it easy. I'll get you into Hunza!"

"*You* get me into Hunza? Why, even the American Ambassador couldn't get permission. Just how can *you* get me into Hunza?"

"Hold on! You tried your way. Did it work? No! We will now try my way."

Art Brevaire sold supplies to the Pakistan government and was a good friend of Colonel Jim Hollingsworth, a Texan, whose job it was to distribute United States appropriations to the Pakistan army. In five years he had passed out five million dollars, and two million more were yet to be distributed. It seemed logical that General Ayub would listen to a request from Colonel Hollingsworth.

"I'll call Colonel Jim first thing in the morning," Art Brevaire said. Then, sticking out his chest, he added: "If you had just known your best friends lived next door and not high-hatted them, you would have been in Hunza a long time ago!"

The following morning at eleven, Art Brevaire phoned that he had arranged for me to meet Colonel Hollingsworth at his office and that a four o'clock appointment for the three of us with General Ayub Khan was to follow at the General's country estate.

The Stateside atmosphere at the Colonel's quarters was refreshing. Colonel Jim simply said, "Hi, Doctor! Come in and let's see what we can do for you."

After hearing my report on what had transpired since my arrival in Pakistan and of the appointment with General Ayub, he appeared confident that something could be accomplished. He invited me to his home for a good American dinner. How wonderful that sounded to me! As the entire staff walked with us to the car, I could see the Stars and Stripes floating in the breeze and, as always, it stirred my emotions.

When I reached the country estate of General Ayub, Art Brevaire and Colonel Hollingsworth were in the garden with a tall, broad-shouldered, handsome man dressed in slacks and a lightweight, white jacket. His slightly graying mustache was neatly trimmed and his features were gently chiseled. I assumed this to be the General, as I had heard he had a great fondness for flowers, and he was displaying the blooms to my friends with genuine pride.

The Colonel made the introductions in English, a language the General speaks with a true British accent. I realized I was in the presence of one of Pakistan's greatest men. General Ayub told us he would like to retire from public life but believed his country would need his services for some time to come. He recognized that many reforms had to be made to elevate the standards of his people.

Colonel Hollingsworth told me later that General Ayub could easily become the leading figure in Pakistan. A year later this prediction came true. The current government was overthrown, and General Ayub assumed the role of leader. Although Pakistan is not a democracy, it does have at the head of government a leader who firmly believes in democratic principles. Eventually the goal will probably be reached. The first act General Ayub Khan performed was to reduce the price of cloth so that the poor people could afford to buy it. A shirt that would cost about $3.00 in America, sold in Pakistan for $7.00. With an average of $30.00 per month income, few people could pay so exorbitant a price.

After a walk around the estate, we sat on a large veranda and were served light refreshments. Gradually Colonel Hollingsworth turned our conversation to the subject of my trip. The General was interested, and listened intently to my purpose in visiting Hunza. He asked many questions and seemed amazed that such a people lived so close to Pakistan.

The General exclaimed, "Dr. Banik, you have a mission. You *must* go to Hunza! I think it can be arranged. In fact, my secret service man is coming in a few minutes, and I will talk it over with him."

In a short time, Colonel Riaz approached. When he saw me sitting with the General he was speechless. Sensing his discomfiture, the General said quietly, "Colonel Riaz, Dr. Banik is planning to go to Hunza. I feel he has an important mission. Do you think we could make arrangements for the trip?"

Colonel Riaz was still in a daze. He could not

quite believe what he heard, and almost stuttered: "Quite so, quite so, Sir. I think the arrangements can be made."

General Ayub then said: "Dr. Banik is in quite a hurry. Do you think we could do it within the next day?"

Colonel Riaz nodded in the affirmative and departed.

The General asked me if I would examine his eyes and, pleased by his confidence in my professional ability, I brought my equipment to his home and conducted the examination. Later General Ayub Khan visited Hunza personally to observe the Hunzakuts' wonderful way of life.

I was now assured of going to Hunza! Before me lay the dangerous and thrilling flight through the mountain passes—the flight Franc Shor had warned me about when he phoned me in Kearney, Nebraska. Would we make it? God would have to be my pilot on this trip.

CHAPTER TWO

THE ROAD TO HUNZA

IT WAS still dark when I arrived at the Rawalpindi airport the next morning. We checked our equipment, secured our tickets and waited to be called. At six o'clock came the announcement that there would be no flight that day because of low clouds in the passes. Passengers were asked to come back the following morning at the same early hour.

There was no choice but to reclaim our baggage and return to the quarters we had left such a short time before. Actually, I didn't mind the delay. Now that my mind was free from worry, my perceptions were sharpened, and I became even more appreciative of my oriental surroundings. I spent the hot afternoon shopping for souvenirs for my family and friends.

The bargaining ritual takes considerable time and much effort, but it is a recognized part of trade in Middle Eastern countries. In the United States, we are accustomed to walk into a shop, examine an article, and pay the price marked on the tag. But that is too simple a procedure for many foreign merchandisers. After an embellished harangue on the merits of the item under consideration, a fantastic price is mentioned in a tone that implies the seller is actually losing money at that figure. That is only the beginning; offers and counter-offers follow, with shouts and gestures, until finally a price is agreed upon. Apparently those people enjoy the struggle of wills.

The next morning the pattern of the day before was repeated: the same waiting for take-off; the same announcement that there would be no flight because of low clouds in the passes.

When I asked the clerk at the airport how long these delays might continue, she smiled and said, "Sometimes for weeks! You see, the atmosphere must be just right. Usually a plane is sent aloft to look down the valley; if it is believed that clouds will not obstruct vision, the signal is given to start the flight. Of course, sometimes the pilots are weary of flying and go up only when they please."

"Load up!" was the welcome message we heard at the third pre-dawn gathering at the airport. A few bright stars still lingered, and there were no clouds. This was it! The flight to Hunza was to begin.

Sight of the two-engined ship rather dampened my enthusiasm, and I wondered fleetingly if our goal would be reached after all. The plane badly needed paint, and its general appearance indicated that it was not going to provide luxury transportation. The interior was in need of dusting, the upholstery was worn, and the windows were smudged. The cabin was dingy and hot. As all the other passengers were natives, we were given the privilege of entering first; we selected a seat that would provide the best possible view.

The engines sputtered into life, enveloping us in a cloud of fumes and white smoke. I had heard

HUNZA LAND

that many Pakistanian pilots could not appreciate why a plane engine should be warmed up and a check-off made before the craft left the ground, and I wondered if ours belonged to that school.

It reminded me of a story told by my friend, Bob Hopper, who supplies tools for Pakistan plane shops. On one occasion the mechanics told him they had plenty of tools, and then displayed a limited assortment of pliers, screwdrivers and wrenches. Noticing the rounded corners of the hexagon nuts on an engine they were repairing, he asked how they knew the nuts were tight. The disconcerting answer was that they *must* be tight if they had lost their edges!

Our pilots, however, did take time to warm up the engines and, as we took off, I peered through the smeared window in search of an opening through the towering mountains that might permit us to enter the Gilgit valley. I could find not a single one! The sun had risen in a cloudless sky as we climbed steadily, heading directly for a high range that had to be cleared as it was the only possible way to reach the valley beyond. Under full

THE ROAD TO HUNZA

power we skimmed the sheer rocks with little space to spare, then descended into the valley at a lower altitude as the cabin was not pressurized.

Seemingly endless peaks cast shadows over the plane as we skimmed so close to the rock sides that a man standing on the wing could have touched them. A steep bank to the left pushed us hard into the seats as we dodged along a precipitous canyon. Then, before we could get our breath, a sharp bank to the right and, again, I strained mentally to push away the mountain that seemed about to tear off the vibrating wing. At the end of each too-short canyon, a quick swerve threw us into consternation as we threaded our way toward Gilgit. These pilots had no modern instruments. They "flew by the seat of their pants" as the air pioneers did. I lost five pounds before we landed.

Such glimpses of the scenery as I dared risk were indescribable. The snow-capped Himalayan peaks sent light flashes into the windows. Far down the mountainsides was the timber line with frequent white torrents of water from melting glaciers contrasting with the variegated greens of the trees.

HUNZA LAND

There were no roads or foot passes, just formidable wilderness.

As we approached Gilgit, the starboard engine sputtered and sent out clouds of smoke. Mahmood closed his eyes and breathed a prayer. But our fear was short lived; the engine soon resumed its steady beat as the fuel line blockage cleared. Word came that we were about to put down. There was no landing place in sight but, with engines idling, altitude diminished and the roar and vibration subsided. Cragged walls reached up for us on either side as we entered a final narrow canyon that demanded continued precise flying skill to avoid calamity.

Then, as the mountains parted, we could see the clearing which was the Gilgit airstrip. The mountains seemed to rise directly from the narrow ledge. As the wheels touched the ground, the plane bounced several times on the rough, dusty airstrip and then came to rest.

Mahmood and I waited for the others to alight before gathering up our belongings and following

THE ROAD TO HUNZA

them through the exit door. It was like stepping into an oven! There seemed to be not a breath of air as the sun beat down in a sizzling 120-degree heat. A small tree, two nondescript buildings, a jeep, and a scattering of airstrip employes completed the scene, except for a tiny village some distance down the dusty road.

As I walked toward the tree in search of some relief from the searing sun, a familiar voice hailed me. "Dr. Banik! How are you?"

I wheeled around to meet the smiling face and outstretched hand of Muzaffar Hussin, the handsome air-conditioning salesman with whom I had spent many agreeable hours in Rawalpindi. He spoke excellent English and could easily have been mistaken for an American.

"Muzaffar, you devil! What are you doing here? How glad I am to see you!"

"Not any happier than I am to see you, Doctor."

"You sure picked the right spot for air-conditioning." I laughed. "You should work on the whole valley! But why are you here?"

"Oh, I travel this route quite frequently. I am hoping to sell an air-conditioner to the political agent."

"Why, that's the man who is supposed to meet me at the airport! He is to arrange the final lap of my trip into Hunza. Where is he?"

"I'm sorry to tell you, Dr. Banik, but General Kiani left for Karachi several days ago and is not expected back for some weeks."

This information was not very encouraging! I had expected the General to have a jeep and driver ready for me on my arrival. Muzaffar flashed a smile and assured me the General had undoubtedly authorized his assistant to take care of all the details. Then he hurried to board the returning plane.

Only a lonely jeep and its driver now remained at the airstrip. Through Mahmood's questioning, the driver agreed to take us to the political agent's home. My clothes were saturated with perspiration in the stifling heat. I had heard the General's place was the only home in Gilgit with American-style

THE ROAD TO HUNZA

bath and sleeping facilities, and I had looked forward to a comfortable stay under his roof, for I sorely needed a bath and a good night's rest before tackling the Himalayas. But this was not to be.

The agent's assistant regretfully announced that I would not be permitted to stay the night as General Kiani had a daughter and allowed no one to enter the house when he was away from Gilgit. When I asked about my jeep and guide, he professed ignorance of the arrangements. The services of a jeep he added, were difficult to obtain because most of these vehicles were used to earn high returns in hauling gasoline. However, he promised to get in touch with me as soon as he could locate one.

At the moment, something to eat and a place to sleep were more important issues. Our driver took us over a winding, dusty road to the lodge of the Northern Scouts, who patrol the Himalaya region around Gilgit to keep the many troublesome tribes under control. The lodge was a colorful building on the side of a hill, surrounded by a lawn kept

HUNZA LAND

green by adjacent irrigation ditches. A green thatched roof and a large front porch enhanced the building, which seemed deserted.

Inside, however, several men were gathered around a large table having lunch. They greeted me cordially and assured me that my requirements for food could be taken care of easily. As to lodging, they promised a room but no bedding; of course, I could use my sleeping bag. The room was small and dark, but there were American pin-ups on the walls, and a low-wattage bulb glowed feebly in the ceiling. Obviously, someone had left it hurriedly to make accommodations for me.

At the lunch table was a group of British officers just returned from climbing Mt. Rakaposhi, the third highest mountain in the world—a peak I was to pass on my way to Hunza. The men spoke enthusiastically of the stamina of the Hunzukut porters who had carried prodigious loads up the mountainsides, helping to make this twenty-fourth attempt successful.

The British climbers were waiting here, hoping to get permission to view Mt. Rakaposhi from the

THE ROAD TO HUNZA

north side. They had not the slightest idea when permission would be given. The complications of getting permits are illustrated by the fact that these British climbers had received permission to *ascend* the mountain on the south side, but now had to get permission to *view* the peak from the north side.

Red tape is not confined to Pakistan, however; the same difficulties are encountered throughout all Eastern and Middle Eastern countries. Document after document must be passed from official to official before a final permit of any kind is granted. No one seems to be in authority, yet everyone can delay any measure.

Although that was one of the hottest nights I ever experienced, I was buoyed up by a message I had received late in the afternoon. The political agent's assistant had secured a jeep and a driver for me, and they would be ready early next morning. The fee had been arranged at 300 rupees (about $65.00). During the sweltering hours before departure I continually wrapped wet towels around my head for some measure of relief, and managed to get a few winks of much needed sleep. Mahmood, in true native fashion, had slept somewhere in the village, and I had to scout for him next morning to make an early start.

The tortuous trail into Hunza lay ahead. This portion of the journey would put my physical capabilities to the test.

As we began to load the jeep, I wondered fleetingly if I was up to the ordeal. Sixteen suitcases and boxes were loaded upon the tiny vehicle, and I wondered whether there would be space left for the driver, Mahmood and myself. After we were finally wedged in, however, the five men who had hovered about during loading clambered aboard! I will never know how they managed to hang on. I was informed that these men would be needed to help push the jeep up the winding cliffs, build up washed-out roads, clear rockslides and put rocks under the wheels. The last was to be an aid to the almost negligible brakes!

At last we threaded our way out of Gilgit. The town seemed busy. On both sides of the dusty main street, where most business was conducted, small, unpainted, open-front booths hopefully offered

THE ROAD TO HUNZA

bolts of colored cloth, curry powder in pottery jars, candles, rock salt in coarse sacks, and a miscellany of other merchandise used in the daily life of the people. Peddlers were hawking their wares, and unceasing bargaining was going on animatedly. Children were everywhere.

After a few miles of dusty road, the jeep approached the long, extremely narrow, wooden suspension bridge which spanned the rushing, noisy Gilgit river. About two-thirds of the way across the bridge, a scrawny little old woman with a heavy bundle on her back glanced fearfully over her shoulder and scuttled along, trying to beat us to the end of the span. The driver gleefully drove close behind her, blasting his horn in derision. The war between the aggressive motorist and the hapless pedestrian seems to be universal.

The mountains rose almost vertically, and the road along the riverbank was constructed by hand labor to circumvent huge boulders. There was no vegetation—not even a thistle—and the barrenness was appalling in a searing 120 degree heat, with not a cloud in the sky. The jeep had no top and perspiration dropped steadily from the bandline of my helmet into my lap.

The driver and the other men kept up a deafening chatter as we rattled along the narrow path and around hairpin turns. There was no space to pass another vehicle, so that an oncoming jeep or caravan would have presented a problem. That apparently didn't bother my driver in the least. Driving with one hand and holding a cigarette jauntily in the other, he turned his head frequently to chat with his companions in the rear. Mahmood, who sat on a gasoline can, looked at me with a wild expression. "No like this way to ride!" he shouted above the rattle of the jeep and the roar of the river.

Super-low gear was called into service as we started a climb impossible without four-wheel drive. With all wheels spinning in the dusty sand, we sometimes scarcely moved. The men jumped off and pushed, and eventually we reached a crest which was a forerunner of many more to come. The radiator was nearly dry; we took a breather to refill it from the river. The oppressive heat was

THE ROAD TO HUNZA

not conducive to tarrying so we pushed along, always in danger of toppling over a dizzying chasm.

The driver was cross-eyed, but perhaps this was an advantage after all! It seemed he could watch the road with one eye and glance up the mountain at the ascending trail with the other to see if a car or caravan was approaching. However, it was rather disconcerting because, as a practicing optometrist, I knew that true depth perception is impossible with a single eye and that distance cannot be gauged accurately without the use of both eyes. These facts didn't seem to deter my driver's exuberance.

Fear grows and diminishes when one is driving high in the Himalayas along treacherous paths, over shaky galleries, with breath-taking distances visible above and below. When a stretch is comparatively smooth, we lose our apprehensions and view the handiwork of God. How glorious vision can be.

As the book of Proverbs says, "Where there is no vision, the people perish." To be free, we must never believe that the world is bounded by the things we see. If we believed it ended at the mountain wall or at the meeting line of sea and sky, we would be prisoners indeed. Vision dissolves barriers, be they mist or mountain.

"Whoa!" we all yelled in our respective languages. "A washout!"

The road a few feet in front of the bumper was completely gone! We all climbed out to observe the impasse. The guide, pointing to the snow-crowned mountain, said in broken English, "Hot sun melt ice. Water come down fast. Wash out road. Must go fast before more washouts."

His logic was frightening, but how were we to hurdle this barrier? Our extra passengers leaped from the jeep and shucked themselves out of clothes and shoes, ready to tackle the job. The washout was about twenty feet wide, and a foot or more of ice-cold water hurtled along the cut. It was the sudden drop into the wash that worried me, for the jeep would teeter as on a fulcrum if the steep sides were not graded.

Suddenly, out of nowhere, two men appeared carrying shovels and pickaxes. These were Hun-

THE ROAD TO HUNZA

zukuts, sent by the Mir in anticipation of this washout. How wonderful of His Highness to have thought of this detail of my trip! It could well spare us spending an uncomfortable night in the mountains. This was my first opportunity to see demonstrated the fabled strength and stamina of the men of Hunza. I judged one to be about forty years old. The other, with raven black hair and just a suggestion of gray in his beard, seemed around sixty.

It was a revelation to watch these men juggling heavy rocks like medicine balls and hurling them into the stream. They shoveled and scraped at the huge banks until the jeep could make the steep descent. By the time the work had been completed, the water had risen above the level of the stones; but with two men ahead, feeling out the path with their bare feet, the driver was able to inch the sturdy vehicle across, and ascend the opposite, almost vertical bank.

It was now high noon. A glance at the thermometer only added to our discomfort. I thought with yearning of those "unbearably hot" days back in Kearney. How I would have welcomed that temperature now! Five miles ahead lay Chalt—the half-way point from Gilgit to Hunza. That five miles would take about an hour if everything went well.

But everything did not go well. We encountered two more washouts, each more serious than the initial one since the waters were deeper and made it far more difficult to get across. We almost lost the jeep on the final crossing as the overloaded little vehicle balanced precariously on unsteady rocks. But one of the men leaped up on the step, and—by sheer good luck—balance was restored. Even our imperturbable driver momentarily paled, but he was not unnerved.

Our tired party pulled into Chalt some two hours later through a narrow gate with a time-worn sign—"Chalt"—barely legible. The small letters "Rest House" spelled out "welcome relief," and a cabin-styled building with a veranda shaded by an apricot tree held out real promise. Trickling water splashed over a terraced wall to another terrace below.

THE ROAD TO HUNZA

Close by, a large mulberry tree offered juicy black berries on its low-hanging branches, and I picked a couple as we headed toward the veranda. In a few moments my guide brought two pans of washed berries and apricots. We placed them on spread newspapers together with some *chappatis* and egg sandwiches we had brought, and this repast somewhat revived us.

Swarms of flies soon drove us into the building, which was empty except for a table, two chairs and a couch—all covered thickly with dust. But it was a haven of sorts. The guide appeared with hot tea, and as we sipped it gratefully, we talked of the coming thirty-mile trek to Baltit, the capital of Hunza.

Chalt, where we rested, is a shabby little village in Nagir, built at the edge of a fast flowing river, the boundary line of Hunza. The people of Nagir and Hunza are not on friendly terms. Years ago athletic events were staged regularly, but the prowess of the Hunzukuts made the competition ridiculous. The Nagirites were not graceful losers, and the matches were called off by mutual consent.

HUNZA LAND

Although Her Highness, the Rani of Hunza, is a member of the royal family of Nagir, that connection does nothing to improve relations between the two little countries.

Nagirites are a complaining people, indolent and sickly. Their houses are poorly constructed; their fields, inefficiently tilled. Flies and other insects in swarms devour fruits and crops; cattle die; disease is rampant; ambition is wanting. The people bitterly criticize the Hunzukuts because they enjoy a better life, and it is believed that the Hunza good fortune is due to the fact that the sun shines longer on that territory. The Nagirites reminded me of the fable of the grasshopper and the ant. When the sun shines they are idle; when winter winds and snows come, they freeze and starve.

Refreshed from an hour's rest, we left ten rupees in payment for our use of the rest house and settled into our places in the jeep. Then we drove slowly down the narrow, dusty street, sounding the horn as we advanced. Men and boys lined up along the road and raised their hands to their caps in salute as we slowly passed. Our men, proud to be riding

THE ROAD TO HUNZA

on a jeep, saluted in return. We felt like celebrities accepting the acclaim in parades along the streets of New York.

Trading places in Chalt were stone and mud lean-tos with open fronts. Wares included shoes, clothing, beads, simple hardware, and native-made items such as beaded scarfs and crude jewelry.

As we left the town behind, the road became much rougher and narrower, and slow driving was imperative, although we were anxious to reach our next destination before nightfall. The brakes were faulty, and the driver had to gear down quickly at times to avoid catastrophe.

We began the long climb toward the 15,000 foot elevation we would have to clear before we could begin the descent into Hunza. Occasionally the engine failed, and the jeep rolled backward until the men jumped off and slipped rocks under a rear wheel. These stalls were dangerous because the narrow ledge on which we drove hung perilously at dizzy heights. Many times after a stall we labored up a particularly steep rise on foot rather than risk an uncontrollable slideback.

HUNZA LAND

Adding to my distress was the driver's habit of gesticulating with both hands when calling attention to a point of special interest. Each time, Mahmood grabbed the wheel, and we all shouted imprecations at the driver in our respective tongues. I didn't understand what the others said, but what I said had a salty American meaning I wish he could have appreciated.

At one sharp turn around a high overhanging cliff, Mahmood shouted, "Look! The old Marco Polo Trail!" Halfway up the mountainside was visible a thin line which was, indeed, the famous route that Marco Polo followed centuries ago. According to legend, it was he who taught the warriors of Hunza the game now known as polo. It is the national game of Hunza, as popular with the people as baseball is in the States. There is also a breed of sheep named after Marco Polo.

Centuries ago, China paid tribute to Hunza so that Chinese caravans might pass unmolested by the fierce and mighty Hunzukuts of old. They scaled the high peaks and hurled huge boulders down on the Chinese with the result that the hapless

THE ROAD TO HUNZA

caravans hurtled into the chasms hundreds of feet below, and the Hunzukuts recovered the plunder at their leisure. Even armies could not conquer the narrow passes. Eventually, the Hunzukuts returned to their major pursuit, agriculture, and for the past several hundred years they have been a peace-loving nation.

The trail was a twenty-four inch path. Too often, a sure-footed burro would slip on its soft edges and plummet to the rocks below, dragging with him all the others which were tied together in the train. I saw a similar disaster almost happen before my eyes. When we stopped to allow a train of heavily laden burros to pass, the bulky pack of one bumped the jeep. The burro's hind foot slipped off the edge, and only a quick grab of the beast's tail by one of the caravan drivers averted catastrophe on the jagged boulders below. It is not uncommon in these mountains to look down and see the mangled remains or the skeleton of a burro, sent to its death by a sudden gust of wind, a rockslide or a soft edge.

As we made a sharp turn, Mt. Rakaposhi in all

HUNZA LAND

its shining splendor came into view. Here, before my incredulous eyes, was the storied ice-capped Queen of the Himalayas—the 25,500-foot mountain, third highest in the world, that is the most desired goal of climbers and photographers all over the globe. The Hunza entry ban makes even the sight of this peak a rare privilege for the outsider. Twenty-three harrowing, unsuccessful attempts had been made to reach the top of Mt. Rakaposhi before the intrepid British climbers I had met at Gilgit finally succeeded.

Mt. Rakaposhi could rightfully be called "Hunza Mountain" because its greatest beauty can be seen only from the Hunza side. This is why the British climbers wanted to get permission to enter Hunza even though they had already conquered the peak from the other side. On moonlight nights, the bright Himalaya moon beams on Rakaposhi's ice-blue sides, lighting the whole valley with an enchanting fluorescent glow.

Mahmood, the camera expert, was so stunned that his voice was husky as he murmured, "I take picture." He took a dozen marvelous color shots

THE ROAD TO HUNZA

which I shall always enjoy, but my memory always goes back to that first moment with God's awesome monument in towering stone.

Reluctantly, we resumed our places in the jeep, hoping to reach Hunza before dark. Now our descent became as abrupt as the climb had been to the 15,000-foot altitude. Although we were eager for our first sight of the Hunza valley, it was impossible to hasten our pace. The road, indeed, seemed to be worse than it was on the ascent, and some turns were so sharp that they could not be negotiated in the customary fashion. It was necessary to drive to the chasm edge, place rocks in front of the wheels to prevent sliding over, then back and turn several times. In places the road could not be seen over the radiator, and we found it wiser to walk. Rockslides were more frequent now, and sudden gusts of wind kept us close to the cliff walls. As shadows deepened, cool breezes from Mt. Rakaposhi gave us new vigor to press on at maddening slow speed.

Around one sharp turn Hunza lay before our eyes—a long, narrow valley hemmed in by towering

HUNZA LAND

mountains on all sides. Far below, the river, sunk in rock banks, snaked its way. Small terraced fields, in varied shades of green and yellow, spotted with the darker foliage of fruit trees, rose in tiers toward the base of the mountains. Springing from the highest fields, sheer rock walls that reached thousands of feet toward the sky fenced in the fabled valley of Hunza. Balboa, first viewing the vast Pacific, could not have been more enchanted.

A chugging jeep broke the silence as it threaded its way toward us up the narrow mountain road. We waited, for we dared not meet it on the way down. Then, like an oversized beetle climbing out of a sand hole, it spun its way up to our narrow ledge and stopped in a cloud of dust. It sported a huge license plate bearing the word "Hunza," but the plate carried no numerals.

Two men alighted and approached us. The younger introduced himself in excellent English. "I am the Mir's uncle, Prince Khan, and this is Sultan Ali, school teacher of Hunza. We have come to welcome you to our country. The Mir was concerned about your trip because there were so many

THE ROAD TO HUNZA

washouts, and he alerted his men along the way to help you. We are glad you have had a safe trip and, from now on, we will take care of you."

After thanking the Prince for his courtesy and concern, my curiosity got the better of me. "You say you are the Mir's *uncle*? May I ask how old you are?"

"Seventeen."

"Then how old is the Mir, if it is not too personal a question?"

"Forty-eight."

"How does it happen that *you* are *his* uncle?"

This question brought a smile to Prince Khan's face, displaying a set of beautifully shaped, white teeth. "You see, Dr. Banik, my father was seventy-five years old when I was born, and I have younger brothers and sisters."

This was my first experience with the amazing virility of the Hunzukuts. I later learned that it is quite common for children to be uncles or aunts of much older people.

We began the trip down the narrow road toward Aliabad. From there we would travel to Baltit, the capital of Hunza. According to the guide, the trip would take at least three hours, and it was now four o'clock. The road down was so steep, with so many hairpin turns, that—with worry over our poor brakes—we had little opportunity to view the scenery. Holding on kept us occupied, as the wheels sent rocks and gravel rolling off the path into the chasms below.

What a blessing to reach the valley and look up toward the hair-raising trail we had just traversed. There was now time to look about. Water trickled and splashed everywhere. Irrigation ditches were full to overflowing; some terraces were almost completely under water as preparations for the next crop began. Although it was early July, some threshing had already been done. The Hunza growing season is the same as ours in the States, but their crops mature faster, allowing for a second planting each year.

Most of the homes are built in clusters or communities, patterned after the feudal system where the fields surround the villages. Because of the small area of the valley, land for raising food is at a pre-

THE ROAD TO HUNZA

mium. Consequently, homes do not have spacious yards. The flat roofs of the houses are used as congregating places and to dry fruits and vegetables. The terraces, cultivated for producing crops, are owned by the people, and generally are located at a considerable walking distance from the owners' homes.

Some curious children watched us as we approached, and then quickly disappeared. A few boys remained beside the road and raised their hands to their caps in the customary Hunza salute. A few men, too, were curious to see the American doctor, wondering if his arrival might change the routine of life in this secluded country.

As we reached the countryside beyond Aliabad, I paid particular attention to the terraces for which Hunza is famous. Some of them are fifteen to twenty feet high, and all of them are built of stones, chinked with smaller stones. They are then leveled, covered with soil, planted and irrigated. It was a prodigious project that obviously had taken centuries to complete. I could readily understand from seeing them why the Hunzukuts are called the "greatest engineers without mathematics."

It was obvious that Hunzukuts of all ages are industrious. Children were picking black and red cherries, apples and apricots from laden trees. Girls with large baskets on their backs gathered twigs and brush for firewood. Men and women worked in the fields.

Their homes are generally two storied. The upper level is used for spring and summer living, and the lower story for virtual winter hibernation. Little wood is available for use in building.

My guide pointed to a solidly built stone structure which he said was one of the new schools established in every village and financed by education funds from the late Aga Khan. My interest in another structure, built on a mound high up the mountainside, prompted the guide to say: "That is the palace of the old Mirs. It was a Hunza stronghold that was never captured in over six hundred years. His Highness will undoubtedly take you through this old palace."

I was struck by the fact that there are no insects

THE ROAD TO HUNZA

in Hunza—a sharp and pleasant contrast to the plague of bugs we fought off in the countries on the other side of the mountains. I noticed, also, that there are no dogs, cats or chickens.

"Dogs need food," my guide explained, "and we do not have much of it. Cats eat mice, but we have no mice. Chickens scratch up our fine gardens, so we have no chickens. And, of course, our Moslem religion forbids us to eat pork, so we have no pigs." He laughingly added, "You see, Dr. Banik, we have a very peaceful country."

I could have remarked that they also had a clean country. Everything seemed immaculate. There were no papers, cigarette butts, beer cans, rubbish or weeds, not even a billboard.

The evening air had become delightfully cool, and many Hunzukuts sat on the terraces enjoying a respite from the day's work. Pretty children stood in our path, then nimbly scooted to either side. On one occasion the jeep driver stopped abruptly because a little boy refused to move, even after my guide spoke rather sharply to him. I caught the lad's eyes as they looked into mine, smiling and intense, then back to the guide with frightened determination.

"What does he want?" I asked Prince Khan.

"He wants to shake hands with you."

"By all means have him come up. I shall be happy to shake his hand."

My guide nodded, and the lad came forward, hesitant yet eager. He saluted rapidly, repeating the words, "Salaam alaikum, Sahib; Salaam alaikum, Sahib."

"Wa-alaikum salaam," I repeated as I reached down to shake the quivering little hand.

He grinned delightedly, not knowing exactly what to do or say. Cheers of approval rang out along the terraces, and the people seemed pleased.

Next I experimented with a little of the Urdu language I had learned in Pakistan, "Mirbonnie sa ao jeep! (Kindly come in jeep!)"

He understood and climbed nimbly into the vehicle to sit proudly on my lap. I told the driver to start, holding my new-found Hunza boy in my arms. His clothes were dusty (and so were mine);

THE ROAD TO HUNZA

his little face was grimy, and a damp, warm towel would have worked wonders. But his large brown eyes sparkled in a velvety smooth face beneath a remarkably thick shock of black hair. I could feel his heart racing as he waved to his friends along the way.

CHAPTER THREE

INTRODUCTION TO HUNZA

The Mir's palace came into view as we rounded the sharp corner of a dike. It is a large, substantial structure of wood and stone, extensively landscaped with flowers, hedges and trees. Near by are the guest house, tennis courts and a large swimming pool. Tall poplars whispered in the cool breeze as our jeep wheeled into the courtyard.

As we alighted, a door on the balcony opened, and a distinguished figure in a brocaded robe, white slacks and karakul cap descended the steps and strode toward me, holding out his hands in smiling welcome.

"Dr. Banik, I'm very happy to meet you. I am

Prince Ayash Khan, brother to his Highness. Welcome to Hunza."

While the Prince was greeting me, the others of the royal family filed down the steps, and I was presented to His Highness, Muhammad Jamal Khan, Ruler of Hunza State.

I could not conceal my joy at the culmination of my twenty year's dream! Rushing forward with outstretched arms, I embraced His Highness, and we stood silent for a moment in mutual thanks that our long-promised meeting had been accomplished.

Then, in flawless English, the Mir said: "I feel honored to be in your presence. I knew through your letters that you were my brother. Welcome to Hunza and to our humble hospitality." Then, turning, he said, "This is Her Highness, the Rani, our most beloved."

She nodded, smiling, and in a low voice said, "Welcome, Dr. Banik."

Her Highness was dressed in a colorful native costume. She was beautiful, her fair complexion contrasting with her black hair which was covered with a flowing white scarf. Her large eyes twinkled

INTRODUCTION TO HUNZA

and her beautifully curved lips were shaded with American lipstick. She was, indeed, a queen.

I then had the pleasure of meeting the other members of His Highness' family. Prince Ghazanfar, twelve-year-old heir to the throne, looked like an American boy. His haircut, clothes, manner and conversation were typical of our youths. This is not strange, because American tutors had been with all of the Mir's children for the past five years. The younger brothers, Princes Amen Khan and Abbas, and five little princesses—Nilofar, Malika Hussn, Mehr Ul Jamal, Fauzia, and Azra—were duly presented. They were all charming children. Princess Duri Shahwar, a married daughter of the Mir, was not present.

His Highness, appreciating that I was tired from the trip, suggested we have refreshments on the balcony before I was shown to my quarters.

Steep wooden steps on the outside of the palace led directly to a magnificently furnished sunroom with a curved glass wall through which the Mir could survey his kingdom. A rich Persian rug covered the floor. The comfortable, family atmosphere was heightened when the younger children grouped themselves in a semicircle at my feet. The scene was reminiscent of a similar one in Rodgers and Hammerstein's *The King and I.*

When I expressed my enthusiasm for the beauty of the Mir's country, he smiled gratefully.

"Thank you," he said. "Your praise makes me feel very humble. I have heard so much about America that it is my greatest dream to visit your country. Maybe, soon, my Rani and I can make this dream come true. We had the opportunity in 1956 when Lowell Thomas, Jr., invited us to New York to see the premiere of Cinerama,* but I was unable to take advantage of his generosity at that time."

I could see the Mir was honored to have Hunza featured in the Cinerama film, and I assured him that hundreds of thousands of Americans would be thrilled by the beauty and wonders of his country. This so pleased the Mir that he translated our re-

---

* *Search for Paradise,* produced and directed by Lowell Thomas, Jr., and released in 1958.

Art Linkletter briefs me on my trip to Hunza.

The *"printing press" of* Hilal, *a Pakistan Government newspaper. It is actually handwritten by the scribes sitting along the wall.*

A Pakistan cloth factory, showing a worker designing an intricate pattern for the looms. Most cloth in these factories is made of rayon.

A Pakistan bazaar offering many items, from coarse wool to antiques.

A snack bar outside a bazaar. Strips of meat are wound around iron poles, then toasted like marshmallows.

A tanga, a common mode of travel in Pakistan.

The plane flight from Rawalpindi, Pakistan, to Gilgit is considered the most thrilling and hazardous flight in aviation history.

Getting started for Hunza are six men and sixteen suitcases in a jeep that had poor brakes, a poor battery and a wild-eyed driver.

The author and a Hunza guide stop beside the rushing Hunza River at the start of the trail into Hunza. Their famous terraced gardens seen high up into the mountains.

Mt. Rakaposhi, 25,550 feet high, the third highest mountain in the world.

The uncle of the Mir of Hunza escorting the author to the six-hundred-year-old stronghold in the distance.

INTRODUCTION TO HUNZA

marks to his Rani, who spoke a few words of English but could not follow a conversation. The Rani beamed with delight and smiled approval as she poured hot tea into priceless, fragile china cups.

"We must talk more about this later," the Mir suggested, "but now you must be tired. This tea will refresh you. A servant has already unpacked your belongings, and he will remain with you to see that all of your needs are satisfied."

The mint-flavored herb tea was, indeed, refreshing. However, the prospect of a bath and clean clothes seemed wonderful, and, after a third cup of tea, I asked to be excused.

The guest house stood on a huge granite boulder. Wooden steps led to a balcony which skirted a comfortable living room and bedroom, with lavatory accommodations adjoining. The European-style appointments were attractive, and there were fresh flowers in the rooms.

An hour later, refreshed and rested, I joined the royal family. Soon we were seated at the dining table. The evening meal consisted of fresh and dried fruit and nuts, curry and rice, *chappatis* with butter, fruit jam and hot tea. Everything was delicious and satisfying.

As dinner progressed, the Mir smiled and said: "We have imported many foods in expectation of your visit, Doctor, but I hope you will also enjoy the simple Hunza food which has sustained our people through the centuries and has kept them the healthiest people in the world."

"Your Highness," I answered, "I came here with the express purpose of eating your food, living your way of life and listening to your teachings. Your way is to be my way. I come as a humble student, with many questions and perplexities. Although my country is considered one of the most advanced, many vitally important questions are still unanswered. I hope some of these answers may be found here in Hunza."

The Mir listened with complete attention. Then, after a thoughtful pause, he said: "As brothers we must help each other. Perhaps a study of our simple ways may unlock great truths. We have always thought it was from America that we must learn.

INTRODUCTION TO HUNZA

You have progressed rapidly in every field, but we have followed our own mode of life for centuries."

As we had dined much later than is customary in Hunza, it was soon time to retire. On this, my first night in the Hunza valley, a bright moon, shining on the icy sides of Mt. Rakaposhi, bathed the entire valley in an ethereal glow of sufficient brightness for me to identify whitewashed houses miles away. Since the Hunzukuts retire early, not a light was visible, and the valley seemed to be an unpopulated portion of another world.

Silence was absolute; no night birds, no dogs barking, no squealing brakes, no honking horns. The thought came to me that for millions of years those towering mountains had protected this same tiny valley—and that for 2,000 of those years they had preserved a civilization from the ravages of hostile neighbors, permitting the development of a hardy, disease-free people unique in their enjoyment of an unparalleled life span. Was there a reason? What could it be?

Lost in thought, I had not noticed my attendant standing motionless in the shadow of the veranda.

An inviting bed was ready for me, with the white sheets turned back. My pajamas were laid out, and a pot of hot tea stood on the bedside table. I was tired, yet very excited.

The Hunzukuts' early rising custom suited me exactly, for I was eager to begin my first full day in the valley. After enjoying the hot tea served in my room, I stepped out on the veranda and realized that the charm of the previous night was equaled by morning beauty. Mt. Rakaposhi's top was crowned in sunlight, and the air was cool with a slight breeze. Men, women and children were already at their tasks. I could see cattle and sheep grazing high up the mountainsides on green patches kept lush by waters trickling down from summit snows.

I was greeted by the Mir, his Rani, and Prince Ayash as I appeared for breakfast at seven. The Mir told me that all Hunzukuts arise at five in the morning, generally take a short nap in the afternoon, and retire about nine in the evening. This

INTRODUCTION TO HUNZA

custom permits hard work, yet assures ample rest.

Breakfast was served in the dining room, with places set on a large table covered by an exquisite lace cloth. The meal included a variety of fruits—apples, apricots, cherries, peaches—with nuts and raw vegetables. The warm dish was dried apricots (soaked in apricot-seed oil until soft) and home-ground oatmeal which had been prepared with cream to lessen cooking time. The tea served was a combination of mint, alfalfa leaves and herbs.

The Mir had planned a visit to a council meeting, talks with the people in the fields and in their homes, and a performance of Hunza's six-hundred-year-old tribal sword dance. Mahmood, of course, was to accompany me with his photographic equipment.

As there was plenty of time before we were due at the council meeting, we settled in comfortable chairs on the balcony, and I eagerly listened to the Mir's fascinating stories.

His Highness told me of the days before the jeep, the telephone and the airplane were known

HUNZA LAND

here. Then messages were delivered on foot over almost impassable mountain trails, often only eighteen to twenty-four inches wide.

"Our men do not know what fatigue is in terms of their daily hard work," His Highness said. "Only with extreme exertion do they feel any tiredness, and then for just a short time." He pointed to an old-fashioned piano which had belonged to his grandfather. "Twenty men—ten at a time—carried that heavy instrument sixty-five miles over the nearly impassable terrain of the Himalayas!"

I was told that an average man of Hunza at the age of eighty or ninety can walk the sixty-five miles to Gilgit and back, carrying a load, and then return to his regular work immediately without any rest. In former days, the Mir's messengers preferred to run rather than ride horseback. They kept up a steady trot around the clock, stopping only briefly for short rests and food. On their return, they required only their usual amount of rest.

Hunza men are straight and tall, broad-shouldered, deep-chested, slim-wasted, and heavy-legged. They walk erect with a smooth, effortless glide that

INTRODUCTION TO HUNZA

can be identified as far as it can be seen. For centuries, Hunzukuts have been known as the most efficient porters obtainable; they carry the heaviest loads, and they appear to be always good natured and uncomplaining. When resting, they seldom take off their heavy packs.

As an illustration of the Hunzukuts' endurance, Franc Shor tells this story in an article on Hunza in the *National Geographic Magazine* written in 1953. Shor had always wanted to hunt the famed Marco Polo sheep that graze at high altitudes. He was granted his wish and accompanied a hunting party on a search that led to an altitude of 18,500 feet. Although he was in excellent physical condition, Franc found he was no match for his Hunzukut companions, who stopped frequently to allow him to rest. Two trackers ranged far ahead, and although they traveled three times the distance the main party covered, they did not seem to tire. Eventually two rams were shot, and it took the trackers two hours of rugged climbing to recover the carcases although the sheep lay only about a quarter of a mile away on a direct line. They brought back only the carcases, but readily offered to make a second arduous climb to recover the heads as trophies for Shor, while he and the others started back down the mountain. It took six hours to make the descent, and shortly after they reached the base camp the trackers came in carrying the heads and carcases of the two Marco Polo sheep. Neither man seemed to be at all fatigued.

The Mir chuckled at his recollection of the event. "Franc and Jean Shor are among the finest people I have met," he said. "I am sorry I will miss them on my trip to America. They will be away on an assignment. But I have a gift for them—a baby male Marco Polo sheep!" He glanced out the window and pointed to the top of a very high mountain. "We keep the sheep fenced in up there."

I was curious to find out how the animal was obtained.

"Thirty minutes after a Marco Polo lamb is born," the Mir explained, "it is as agile as its mother and must be captured within fifteen minutes. The only way to do this is for men to hide behind rocks a considerable distance away and train their telescopes on the sheep. As soon as the lamb is born, the hunters rush to capture it." The Mir stated that he hopes to secure a female sheep for Mr. Shor and that they both will be donated to a museum—the only ones of their kind in captivity.

I then asked His Highness if his men had ever encountered one of the famous "Abominable Snowmen."

"Yes, we have seen some," he replied, "but our men were no match for them. They disappeared like flashes. They were much taller than our men, shaggy and very muscular. The peculiar thing they noticed was the eyes, which seemed very close together, almost like one eye instead of two. Of course, the men were very frightened, so I don't know just what to believe."

Queried as to whether he had ever had any personal experiences that called for undue exertion, the Mir thought for a moment.

"Maybe what seems undue to you may be just natural for us," he said. "Yes, you may put it that way. I have had many such experiences, as I hunt a great deal. I enjoy hunting and consider it good sport. Sometimes I hunt for weeks at a time. I have some twenty-five high-powered rifles and guns. Hunting Polo sheep is my favorite sport, next to polo and archery.

"However, I did have an experience you may enjoy hearing. I had to make an important trip to Gilgit, a distance of sixty-five miles, in the days when there were no roads, just the old trail. As I had to be there on that same day, I started early in the morning with my best horse, traveling a distance that would take a burro three days. I wore out two horses, but I kept my appointment. I was not unduly fatigued. You see, Dr. Banik, we live here; it is natural for us to do these things. When we see a mountain, we climb it. If a boulder gets in the way, we move it. If a mountain stream washes away the trail, we rebuild it. We just go on."

Here was a philosophy that could well be copied. There was no fear—no fear of distance, height, danger, fatigue. How different from our reactions! I can hear my neighbor scream, "Now Junior, if you lift that pail of water you'll strain yourself."

INTRODUCTION TO HUNZA

And, "Put on that coat or you will catch a deathly cold." Or, "Please go to bed or you will be so tired in the morning you'll get sick." And Junior is invariably tired in the morning, and really doesn't feel well. He carries half-pails of water to avoid strain; he bundles up warmly for fear he may catch cold. Thus, little by little, fear strikes Junior down, and during a lifetime he builds up a myriad of fears that all become real to him. Financial worries, physical disabilities, old age—with the proper frame of mind he will be sure to "enjoy" all of them.

At ten o'clock that beautiful morning, we were ready to begin the long, steep climb to the old palace of the former Mirs. His Highness asked me to start without him, as he wanted a little time to dress for the occasion.

Guide and cameraman were on hand, and we started out briskly. The cobblestone road rose at a steep angle, and I found walking difficult. As the rise became steeper, I frequently suggested stopping so that I might recover my breath. I rather hoped the elders accompanying me would think I was suggesting the stops out of deference to their age, but they seemed to be completely at ease, without any sign of heavy breathing or perspiration. My cameraman, thirty-three years old, was puffing and sweating profusely.

After several hairpin turns, always going up sharply, we ascended rock steps to an entrance in an adobe wall which surrounded a small, dusty yard. Above was the windowless west wall of the palace. A narrow door—the only opening in the wall—led to steep, coarse marble stairs with handrails made of wood polished smooth by hands that had slid along them for some six hundred years.

The palace was actually three stories high, but the top story was of smaller dimensions and set back to afford a considerable area of flat roof. This was where council meetings were held. The double walls of the massive building were constructed of logs, with the wide space between the walls filled with rocks and rock-hard mud; the outside surface was adobe covered and at one time had been whitewashed.

As I did not wish to seem out of breath when

INTRODUCTION TO HUNZA

I stepped out on the rooftop to greet the assembled elders, I rested a few minutes in a small, dark room. After all, I was representing America and I wanted to make a dignified entrance. When I walked out on the flat roof, the elders clapped their hands, rose to their feet, and then sat down cross-legged. The elders offer a striking picture as they sit in deliberation, their beards dyed flaming red as badges of authority and seniority. The council members in the first row range in age from seventy to ninety years; those in the second row can boast ninety to one hundred five years of age.

On a small carpeted throne sat the Mir of Hunza, beautifully attired in his ceremonial robes, plumed cap, and ancient sword. I had enjoyed a fifteen-minute start and had outdone myself in order to precede the Mir to the palace; but there he sat, appearing cool and comfortable, with no sign of fatigue.

When I asked him if he had come by horseback, he replied laughingly, "Why, of course not! I *walked*—it was just a short jaunt." Later I found that it took me nearly two steps to match his smooth stride, though he was slightly shorter than I!

The Hunzukuts have a very democratic form of government, although the state is ruled by the Mir, who has the power of life or death over his subjects. A committee of elders representing every village settles such problems as may arise. The Mir acts as advisor. Thievery, acts of violence and murder are unknown in this remarkable land (there are no soldiers or police), and the main problems of contention involve water rights. The most serious penalty that can be imposed is banishment from Hunza.

The mock trial, staged for my benefit, illustrated the points about Hunza justice that His Highness had highlighted for me. The Mir rose solemnly and raised his arm to the plaintiff on the right; then to the defendant on the left. Each man bowed gracefully toward his ruler, then looked at the other, waiting for the signal to begin the arguments. They were tall men in their middle seventies, wearing long, flowing robes and homespun caps with rolled brims.

A nod from the Mir released a torrent of fast talk and excited chatter accompanied by a remarkable

INTRODUCTION TO HUNZA

repertoire of gesticulations. In about ten minutes, the Mir nodded. Silence was immediate. His Highness looked toward the elders as if to read their decision. He then glanced at the plaintiff, and the elders nodded.

"You win," announced the Mir. "Case dismissed."

The disputants embraced, shook hands, smiled and seated themselves. Simple justice is achieved quickly in Hunza courts—no expense, no lengthy preparation, no lingering animosity.

It is almost impossible to imagine the existence of a country so free from the disputes, ill-feeling and strife that shake the modern world. The Mir has no bodyguards and needs none, for he has no enemies. His Highness is beloved by the Hunzukuts, and they are his whole existence. The people kiss his hand as he walks by, and they rise as he passes. Each would gladly bring the first fruits of his soil to the Mir before partaking of a single morsel himself.

The Mir of Hunza is, indeed, a loving father to all his subjects. He knows them all by name. And, in the same fashion, Her Highness is adored. She meets with the women and helps them with their problems; and they know they have a loyal friend to whom they can always turn.

As we left the old palace after the mock trial, an accident happened that served to acquaint me both with the stoical nature of the people and the methods with which they cope with inevitable physical misfortunes. Hearing a scream, I turned quickly and was horrified to see a little girl fall some twelve feet to a rocky wall on the terrace below.

The child, who appeared to be about four years old, had been attempting to balance herself on the wall. Men carried the frightened child toward us. Her arm was fractured. One of the elders beckoned to the girl, and she trustingly sat in his lap. I could hear the snap as his gentle fingers set the bone; he then fashioned splints from two pieces of wood. Tearing a cloth into strips, he expertly bound the splints around the arm. The entire procedure took but five minutes.

It was remarkable to me that, during the entire time, the little girl did not utter a sound; there were no tears in her eyes. This was an example of the

INTRODUCTION TO HUNZA

Hunzukuts' ability, from childhood on, to cope with problems without demonstrating fear. The incident was closed without dismay on anyone's part when the father led the child away, uncomplaining.

Naturally, I was impressed by the expedient way in which this emergency case was handled, and asked for further information. Through an interpreter, I gathered that each village has a competent bone-setter, who is authorized to instruct and train others in this art. The technique is seemingly perfect, as I learned on manual examination of the legs and arms of several men who had suffered fractures. Their bones had knitted without evidence of breaks. Splints are generally removed in about one week.

Preparations for the tribal dance were getting under way as we approached an L-shaped, pavilion-type building. Instruments of the eight-piece orchestra were being readied, and the dancers were giving final inspection to their costumes, swords and shields. The orchestra finished tuning up, and the dance was about to begin, when the Mir suddenly exclaimed, "The grounds are too dusty! Let us wet them down." A five-gallon can and an irrigation ditch, about one hundred yards away, provided the means to accomplish this wise suggestion. Of course, Mahmood was ready with his cameras to record the event for television.

As the ground-sprinkling was going on, the Mir turned to me with a smile and said: "When Lowell Thomas, Jr., was here in 1956, he brought two beautiful and charming secretaries with him. He had a tape recorder with lively American dance music, and the secretaries taught us to dance with *them*. It was the first time the idea had been practiced in Hunza. I can say frankly I think your American custom is much more enjoyable than ours!"

Finally, the dancing area was satisfactorily soaked. The sound that came from the clarinets, pipes and drums of the Hunza band, seated in a semicircle on the ground, surprisingly enough turned out to be good dance music, with a strong rhythm that encouraged foot-tapping accompaniment. There actually seemed to be a similarity to the American fox trot, and I imagined I recognized some of the melodies.

INTRODUCTION TO HUNZA

No part of the dance, however, invoked memories of anything I had seen in the States. It began with a thunderous clashing of swords and clanging of shields. As the music became faster, the men leaped high in the air. The tempo became wilder and swifter as the warlike lives of Hunzukut forebears were simulated.

We found it wise to move back as swords swished with dazzling speed. The gyrations continued for half an hour, with strident encouragement from the spectators. Here was the last vestige of ancient Hunza ferocity, when bold warriors protected their homes and loved ones from the onslaught of cruel invaders—a ferocity that preserved this isolated civilization to this day.

When the strenuous dance was finished, I could detect not the slightest exhaustion or heavy breathing among the participants. They looked fresh and ready to continue for hours. Yet, these men had left their hard work to entertain us, and now returned to the fields to continue their labors.

CHAPTER FOUR

HUNZA FARMING AND FOOD

UNDOUBTEDLY the farming methods of the Hunzukuts and the type of food they have eaten for centuries are responsible for the remarkable vigor, long life and freedom from disease enjoyed by this unique race. Their agricultural methods are empirical, not based on scientific study, for they have been followed without deviation for thousands of years.

Terracing makes small flat fields which ascend like steps up the slopes toward the mountains. Sometimes they reach nearly to the timber line. It is staggering to think of the number of man-hours required to break, haul and set in place the countless rocks of all sizes that make possible this remarkable farming system.

Water, of course, is an essential of farming, and the Hunza fields (generally about one-half acre to five acres in area) must be irrigated constantly, especially as two crops are grown each year. The Hunzukuts are fortunate in having a water supply that comes from melting snows high in the mountains. However, the present farmers owe thanks to former generations. Water must be tapped in the mountains and brought down to the fields, and early Hunzukuts laboriously built, with wooden shovels and ibex horn picks, main channels and terrace-irrigating canals which are engineering masterpieces.

The mountain water is rich in minerals and carries to the fields a plant-nourishing silt, which is invaluable in replenishing the growing properties of the soil. Because of the importance of water in the Hunza economy, disputes about this resource comprise the greater part of the court docket the council of elders rules upon. Early in the spring and again before second crops are planted, canal gates (large

HUNZA FARMING AND FOOD

flat stones) are opened and all the terraces are flooded. When the water has been absorbed by the soil, leaving the silt deposit, terraces are plowed and fertilized.

Of course, in agriculture of this kind, soil must be enriched regularly by means other than silt from the mountain waters; indeed, the Hunza soil is almost a manufactured soil. Every solitary thing that can serve as food for vegetables, field crops and fruit trees is diligently collected, stored and distributed in rationed equality over every square foot of the hundreds of terraces. Sunken compost pits are conveniently located, and into them go ashes from cooking and heating fires, inedible parts of vegetables, pulverized animal bones, dead leaves, rotten wood and the collected manure of animals.

The Hunzukuts' idea of returning to the soil everything that comes from the soil is actually comparable to Nature's law as applied in the impenetrable jungle. There is no intrusion of non-living matter in the jungle. Plants, animals, birds, reptiles and insects come into being, live their life span, die and return as life-giving elements to the incredibly fertile jungle soil. It is simply a cycle of life–death–life. Nothing is ever lost; nothing wasted.

Nations not blessed with sufficient arable land to feed their people are forced to adopt a farming system that is kindred to gardening. It is the principle described in the paragraph above—the returning to the soil everything, vegetable and animal, that the soil has produced.

In Hunza this type of "garden farming" has produced a quality of vegetables that cannot be duplicated in any other way. Plant disease and destruction by pests are virtually negligible in Hunza. Is this a reward for repaying in full to the soil what the soil has given to the people?

How different is agricultural practice in Western nations such as ours! Each year, countless tons of life-giving soil are sucked up by the winds and scattered over the landscape to become nothing more than a temporary source of complaint to grumbling citizens who dwell in towns and cities within a radius of hundreds of miles. Water erosion, too, is a scourge which must be paid for in money, time and health. Scientific "medication"—calcium, nitrogen, phosphorus—can never restore the virgin quality of the soil, and we pay dearly through loss of health-giving properties in our vegetables and grains.

What foods are grown by the Hunzukuts in this "nothing lost, nothing wasted" agricultural economy? How do they compare in quality and taste with those we are accustomed to in this country? Is there a relationship between these foods and Hunza health? The answers to these questions open an interesting field of conjecture that could apply importantly to our own life and living habits.

It is surprising how many different food products are grown in this small agricultural area which is limited by towering mountains to a section about sixty miles long and from one to four miles wide.

Grains include wheat, barley, buckwheat, corn, millet, alfalfa and rye.

Seven *fruits* offer ample diversity to the diet: apricots, peaches, apples, cherries, mulberries, watermelons and grapes.

Vegetable requirements are satisfied by potatoes,

tomatoes, carrots, onions, garlic, peas, beans and pulses.

Nuts are restricted almost entirely to walnuts.

Milk, mostly from goats, provides butter and cheese (some of the latter aged to one hundred years!).

Meat is scarce (mostly mutton, beef and wild sheep).

Eggs must be imported for the royal family and wealthy citizens. Chickens are viewed with suspicion because they scratch up precious seeds and crops. As the Moslem faith absolutely prohibits pork, pigs are not in evidence in Hunza.

Although they are Moslems, the Hunzukuts drink a quantity of both white and red wine (local).

I have never tasted fruit so sweet and delicious as that I enjoyed in the Hunza valley! Apricots are one of the staples of the native diet, but the trees are not like the ones we see in our orchards. They are allowed to grow for at least fifty years before the tops are cut off about twenty feet from the ground; then growth continues for an equal period. Thanks to the richness of the Hunza soil and to

HUNZA FARMING AND FOOD

their age, the trunks of these trees match the circumference of forest trees, and production of fruit is prodigious. The importance of the apricot in the Hunza economy is suggested by the fact that the trees are regarded as valuable property which, on the death of the owner, is willed to a favorite son or other relative. To own an apricot tree is an indication of affluence, and the local maidens cast covetous eyes on swains fortunate enough to boast ownership of such a prize.

My first experience with Hunza apricots, fresh from the tree, came when my guide picked several, washed them in a mountain stream, and handed them to me. I ate the luscious fruit and casually tossed the seeds to the ground. After an incredulous glance at me, one of the older men stooped and picked up the seeds. He cracked them between two stones, and handed them to me. The guide said, with a smile: "Eat them. It is the best part of the fruit." The seeds tasted much like almonds—very sweet and oily.

My curiosity aroused, I asked, "What do you do with the seeds you do not eat?"

HUNZA LAND

The guide informed me that many are stored but most of them are ground very fine and the squeezed under pressure to produce a very rich oil. "This oil," my guide claimed, "looks much like olive oil. Sometimes we swallow a spoonful of it, when we need it. On special days, we deep-fry our *chappatis* in it. On festival nights, our women use the oil to shine their hair. It makes a good rubbing compound for body bruises. We also shine silverware with it."

Here, it seemed, was an indispensable item in Hunzukut existence. (I learned later that apricot oil actually will shine silver.) One of the greatest values of the oil is its remarkable richness in the blood stream. Is there a connection with the freedom from circulatory disease that the Hunzukuts enjoy? Remember, their old men can scale high mountains or work vigorously in the fields day after day without thought of heart attacks or strokes. My eye examinations demonstrated remarkably healthy circulatory systems in these people.

Apricots and mulberries are dried in the sun to serve as food when the fresh fruit is not in season.

HUNZA FARMING AND FOOD

Enough of this harvest is put aside for use throughout the fall and winter months. Dried apricots may sound unappetizing to the average person in the United States, but there is nothing unpalatable about this fruit when it is eaten in Hunza.

After the dried fruit has been soaked in water overnight, it resumes its original size and is just as sweet and delicious as the day it was picked from the tree. These apricots, cooked with stone-ground oatmeal and milk and served hot, are the main dish at many a meal. Sugar is unknown in Hunza, and importation of this sweetener is not a problem, because Hunza fruits are rich in natural sweetness. Candidly, I found them somewhat too sweet.

Grains, of course, are eaten in a cooked state by the Hunzukuts. Threshing is done in a slow, primitive way by scattering the stalks on a hard surface and driving sharp-footed animals over them. After endless hours the edible part of the grain is separated from the stalks, which are shaken thoroughly and removed. The usable grain is then ground in stone mills and stored for future use in containers similar to our round grain bins.

HUNZA LAND

The ubiquitous *chappati* is generally made of wheat or millet, baked or deep-fried, and served with accompanying food. They are very tasty, especially in their fancier forms, and their nourishing qualities far outshine those of our bread because the natural goodness is not lost in milling. *Chappatis* can be made of other grains than wheat and millet, and dried vegetables (peas, beans, etc.) are often ground up and used with grains in making this Hunzukut "staff of life."

The important thing about the use of grain in the Hunzukuts' diet is that all the goodness and health-giving properties of the grain are utilized. This is in startling contrast to the way grain is used in the United States. Modern milling processes remove the germ from the grain. The germ, as the name implies, is the small part which gives life to the plant. However, as this germ is oily, it causes stored flour to become rancid and harbor parasites. And, too, it darkens bread, making it unappetizing to many people in "civilized" countries.

This fact was brought home to me with startling clarity when I saw with my own eyes the vigor and

HUNZA FARMING AND FOOD

stamina of the Hunzukuts. These people have never eaten "white" bread from which modern milling methods have robbed the phosphorus, potassium, iron, calcium, manganese and sulphur. The important life-giving substances are found in the germ of the wheat (or other grain), in the brown husk and directly beneath the husk. At least three quarters of the real goodness and fullest nourishment in the grain is lost by our "superior" milling. Of course, it is claimed that *some* of the elements are restored to our flours—but why take them away in the first place?

Vegetables in season are eaten raw by the Hunzukuts. At home we eat a few raw vegetables (as in salads), but these healthy natives prefer the food in its raw state. Here, again, they are smarter than we are. They get the full nourishment of the plant, because it is altered very little in the transfer from soil to table. Even corn on the cob is eaten raw in the milk stage. They soak beans and peas in water for one or two days, and then spread the seeds out on wet cloths in the sun. They are eaten raw when they begin to sprout.

Vegetables are cooked by boiling in covered pots —a method comparable to our steaming. Very little water is used and this is replenished in small quantities as required. The water in which the vegetables are cooked is drunk at the time the food is eaten, or saved for future consumption. This, again, is a wise custom, because much of the food value of the vegetables is concentrated in the water in which they are cooked.

Vegetables, whether eaten raw or cooked, are not scrubbed so thoroughly as is our custom; consequently the vital health-giving skins are eaten— advantageously. About twenty per cent of the food eaten in Hunza is cooked; the balance is eaten in its natural state.

Livestock production in Hunza is severely limited because grass is almost nonexistent, and it is impossible to fatten animals properly. Such pastures as are available are located high in the mountains. Sheep and goats can subsist on less fodder than cattle, and the available supply of leaves and straw produces more milk when fed to these animals. Cows are a rarity in Hunza.

HUNZA FARMING AND FOOD

When an occasional animal is slaughtered, usually in the festival season in winter, every morsel of meat is consumed. Even the vital organs are cooked and devoured. Bones are ground for fertilizer, and the gut is dried for a variety of uses such as thread and instrument strings. Of course, the skins are cured and used as leather.

Meat dishes are predominantly stews, which simmer until tender in large kettles with such whole grains as millet, wheat, barley and corn. During the latter part of the cooking fresh vegetables are added to make a mutton stew, a real treat for the Hunzukuts.

The goat's milk and butter used in Hunza are a far cry from those products we are accustomed to and, frankly, I prefer the taste of ours. Of course, the preservation of milk and butter is a problem in countries without refrigeration of any kind, and Hunza is no exception.

These sturdy people, of necessity, follow the oriental method of separating the milk-fats and boiling them to form *ghee,* which is used as butter. *Ghee* is eaten on their *chappatis,* and is used in some cooked dishes. Both milk and buttermilk are used soured, as they cannot be kept fresh. Nutritionists tell us that the soured milk actually offers advantages over our pasteurized product; many peoples who use soured milk exclusively are noted for their fine physiques, virility and good health.

Perhaps something should be said about the lighter side of eating and drinking in Hunza, and this is as good a place as any to mention the famed Hunza wine which I occasionally sampled with gratifying results. This wine is made from the grapes which grow profusely on vines that climb the terraces and mountainsides in the Hunza valley. The drink is called Hunza Pani—*pani* means "water"—and it has a pleasant, mild taste that belies its potency. Hunza Pani enjoys a reputation in the Middle East, and almost everyone is eager to get it.

When I drank the wine for the first time I found two small glasses more than sufficient. However, when I brought up the subject at the Mir's table, he laughed good-naturedly.

"Do your people ever become intoxicated from drinking Hunza Pani?" I asked.

HUNZA FARMING AND FOOD

He shook his head in the negative.

"Do they drink it freely?" I insisted. "More than two glasses at one time?"

"Why, of course," His Highness assured me. "On festival nights they drink it by the bottle, and every day it is a normal part of their meals."

At my incredulous look, the Mir added, "Perhaps that is why we are known as the healthiest and happiest people in the world!" It is in the drinking of wine and in allowing their women to go about freely that the Hunzukuts differ from the majority of Moslems.

RECIPES

Chappatis—Whole grain flours, or mixed flours of different grains, mixed with eggs, milk, butter, salt, yeast; allowed to ferment two hours; then baked. (About the size of large pancakes.)

Oatmeal and Apricots—Fresh or sun-dried, unsulphured apricots, mixed with apricot-seed oil, until soft, sweet and mushy; then poured over cooked oatmeal to give it sweetness.

Hunza Kalochees—Lamb stew, highly minced, sealed in chappatis; then cooked in apricot-seed oil. (Only on special occasions.)

Apricot Sauce—Sun-dried, unsulphured apricots soaked in water the night before, with added apricot-seed oil; then mixed in a gelatin, until fairly thick. (Used for a dessert.)

Curry and Rice—Lamb stew, highly minced and spiced, poured over salted, cooked rice. (An imported dish, used mostly at the Mir's palace.)

CHAPTER FIVE

HUNZA FAMILIES AND HUNZA HEALTH

THE Hunzukuts are a friendly people, and a cordial welcome awaited me at every home I visited.

Their modest houses are virtually all alike in appearance and construction. All members of the family help in building a house, and neighbors lend their assistance. Sites are dependent on finding a level piece of ground sufficiently large to accommodate the building and a small walled-in yard. Cellars are nonexistent because it is impossible to hollow out the hard rock foundations.

The typical home is two-storied and built of carefully fitted split stones. Wood, of course, is used for such doors as are needed, but there are no windows. All light comes from a square opening in the ceiling of the first floor and a larger opening in the ceiling of the second floor. These openings serve a dual purpose: in addition to supplying light, they provide a vent for smoke. The hearth is built in the exact center of the first floor room, and consists of a shallow hole with a low stone curbing around it. Hard packed earth forms the floors of the Hunzukut home. They are swept frequently. These people are extremely neat and clean.

The main room is about fifteen feet square, and a storeroom adjoins in the rear. At the time of my visit, these storage places seemed well supplied with dried apricots and other dried fruits, apricot oil and seeds, grain of several kinds, baskets of potatoes, and pottery jars of wine. Access to the second story and the roof is by ladders, and the agility with which the natives can run up and down on these precarious footholds is amazing: they even carry bulky loads with no thought of falling.

The second story of the house is used as living quarters in the summer. The roof proves ideal for drying the ever-present apricots and other fruits, and a low wall prevents the wind from blowing the produce away; it also channels rain water into a container on the ground floor. Furniture is simple, usually homemade, and it is scarce because of the shortage of wood. Goats or sheep are penned in the small walled yards, and their manure is added to the compost supply.

Dress is not a problem of the Hunzukut women, and they do not wait breathlessly for the dictates of fashion czars. Many of the women are very good looking, but, good looking or not, they wear shapeless smocks that reach below the knees. The ensemble is completed by baggy trousers. All women, and even the little girls, wear pillbox hats, and any longing they may have for individuality in dress is expressed in the fine, cross-stitched embroidery designs on these hats; bright colors predominate. Two long plaits of hair falling below the little hats identify married women; young girls display just a fringe of hair below the hats and, as they approach marriageable age, the hair is allowed to grow to shoulder length.

All the men wear woolen hats which look some-

HUNZA LAND

thing like generous-sized berets with large, loosely rolled brims running completely around the headgear. These hats lend a rather jaunty appearance when worn at the proper angle. As to clothing, the men's garb does not follow any particular style. In former days, I was told, most men wore long, flowing robes which were rather distinctive. Today, Western garb has been adopted by some of the males, and the combinations worn are less than appealing.

In winter, both men and women wear *chogas*—long cloaks of homespun cloth. These garments, intricately embroidered in bright colors, are a customary gift to guests of the Mir. Several months of painstaking labor are required to turn out these elaborate robes.

I was particularly interested in learning about the children of Hunza, because our problems with the youth of our nation are so much a center of concern. The Hunzukut children are curious about the foreigners who visit their country, and they cheerfully tag along with the visitors if allowed to

HUNZA FAMILIES AND HUNZA HEALTH

do so. However, they stay in the background, and I never witnessed an offensively aggressive or show-off attitude among them.

In a Hunza home, the children accept discipline without argument. Each child has his own duties to perform. Bickering of any kind is not tolerated. Parents seem unconcerned as even the little children climb ladders, scale walls and play on precarious footings. From the time they are able to walk, these children—generally under the tutelage of an older brother or sister—are taught how to handle themselves in the face of hazards that would drive an American parent frantic.

Hunza offers a dangerous playground: high terraces, cliffs and walls, open reservoirs and streams, unguarded flat roofs. Yet one never hears the agitated warnings of a distracted mother to "watch out for this," "be careful of that," "don't fall," etc., etc.

The fact that the Hunzukut male children are nursed by their mothers until the age of three (girls to the age of two) may or may not have any significance in the character and strong bodies of the offspring. However, it is the belief of these people that a long nursing period gives the youngsters the best possible start in life.

It is their home life that has made Hunza children so superior in character. The young Hunzukuts are brought up in an atmosphere of firmness, serenity and good nature. They laugh readily and seem to have a kindly feeling toward everyone. There is no juvenile delinquency in Hunza.

Racial strength is maintained because marriage is not allowed between close relations. It is very unusual for first cousins to marry. Both male and female Hunzukuts are generally married before they reach twenty years of age, and the husbands need never worry about forgetting their wedding anniversaries because all weddings, except those in the royal family, take place on a December day decided upon by the Mir.

Although Hunza parents wield considerable influence in selecting mates for their children, the final choice is actually left to the young folks. Divorce is most uncommon among these tranquil people.

HUNZA FAMILIES AND HUNZA HEALTH

Intervals of two to four years are customary between births in families, yet overpopulation is threatening the state. When a Hunzukut woman becomes pregnant, she sleeps on the "women's side" of the house for two or three years. The people of the valley seem to have settled the proverbial mother-in-law problem in an amicable way. As parents and their married offspring generally live under the same roof, the mother-in-law's status is that of a teacher for the newly married women. The value of her experience in the ways of homemaking is appreciated, and clash of temperaments seems to be unheard of.

Women play an important role in Hunza life, although they cannot inherit land because they are physically unable to do such heavy work as tilling the soil. However, the distaff members of a family can own other property (such as apricot trees), and they have equal authority with the men in family matters. All women, except those of the royal family, move about freely without veils.

Formal education for the male children was recently introduced with a grant from the Aga

Khan. The schools, of course, are housed in primitive buildings, and equipment is limited. Subjects taught include history, geography, arithmetic and languages—Urdu, Persian and English. Burushki, the native language of the people around Baltit (the capital), is not written, and it is not taught in the schools. I am told that Burushki is a very difficult language of unknown origin. Of course, no one can estimate now how proficient the young Hunzukuts will become in absorbing book learning, but the ideal of formal education is a real step forward in this little country.

"Old age" in Hunza is not something looked forward to with dread, but it inevitably comes to every living thing. It amazed me to see the number of older citizens going about their work and showing none of the signs of decrepitude that are so often evident in our country.

In fact, age is given respect in Hunza. The young people look up to senior citizens because they have had years of experience, and the Hunzukut youths are wise enough to take advantage of the advice

HUNZA FAMILIES AND HUNZA HEALTH

the elders give. This respect for elders is instilled into the children from the time they are first able to toddle about.

I am sure the Hunzukuts do not consciously follow any regime designed to insure long life. But they acquire their years gracefully and the wrinkles and gray hairs are held at bay a remarkably long time. I am equally sure that at the ages of forty-five or fifty the Hunzukuts do not suddenly begin a frantic search for elixirs and nostrums that might erase the years. As their homes and gardens are on hilly locations, walking and working in the fields naturally is a part of their daily practice regardless of their age differences. They inhale the pure fresh mountain air and no doubt nature taught them how to breathe correctly, which is so essential to our well-being. The Hunzukuts, consciously or subconsciously, have learned to preserve their bodies and thus live to a vigorous old age. Peace of mind is theirs, also, as hatred, greed, envy and jealousy are foreign to these wonderful people.

Surely there is a lesson here for the people of our

own country who are sufficiently interested in the possibilities of a longer, happier life through following sensible rules for eating and living.

One of my major reasons for wanting to visit Hunza was to find out whether their robust health would be corroborated by evidence of superior circulatory function as revealed by a study of the arteries and veins within their eyes; also, to learn if their eyesight was superior, in general, to that of our population.

Although optometrists do not practice medicine, their knowledge of pathology enables them to refer patients with abnormalities to proper medical authority. In my opinion, comparison of the diameters of the arteries and veins of the eye indicates whether the circulatory system is "in balance" or "out of balance"—whether a person's blood pressure is normal or abnormal. Determination of the color relationship between arteries and veins is also indicative of an individual's condition. For example, if the color ratio between an artery and a corresponding vein is 1:1, a person is healthy (i.e. the artery is a rich red and the vein has a color intensity of equal degree). If the ratio is 1:2 (the vein is two shades darker than the artery), health is somewhat below normal. The average American—including many children—falls into this category. A ratio of 1:3 indicates illness; at approaching death the ratio is 1:4.

Interesting evidence of this theory is supplied by studies made by Dr. Melvin Knisely of the University of Chicago. Dr. Knisely made an exhaustive study of the color changes in the circulatory systems of dying frogs, monkeys and humans, and was able to predict the progression of diseases. As death approached, the toxin-laden corpuscles were unable to pass through the capillaries. Their progress was stopped and their oxygen content was discharged.

As a sticky substance in the blood coated the dying cells, they formed into clusters which the doctor called "blood sludge"—a condition common in fifty diseases. Gradually, the blood flowed more slowly, and the tissues died of asphyxia. "Understanding sludge," Dr. Knisely says, "will make possible a new attack on a whole panorama of human diseases." Photomicrographs of the circulatory systems of frogs, monkeys and humans substantiated the theory. An account of this remarkable discovery appeared in *Life* Magazine, May 31, 1948.

The examinations I made in Hunza of the eyes of people in all age groups indicated that the Hunzukuts have healthy circulatory systems. Their artery-to-vein circumference ratios were, in most cases, perfect or near perfect, and the color ratios could generally be classified at 1:1.

In all respects, the Hunzukuts' eyes were notable. I found them unusually clear; there were few signs of astigmatism; even the oldest men had excellent far- and near-vision—an indication that their crystalline lenses had retained elasticity. Most of our crystalline lenses lose their elasticity in our early forties, and we require bifocal lenses for the remainder of our lives.

Here, I believe, is confirmation of the facts that bodily health can be "read" by a study of the eyes, and that general health promotes eye health. For our own benefit and that of our children, we should resolve that, starting now, we will make the necessary adjustments in our diet to promote the radiant health to which we are all entitled.

The people of Hunza do not rely on drugs. Their blood has attained its vigor-promoting properties solely from the natural foods these people have been growing for centuries on land enriched by returning to the soil everything that is taken from the soil.

Our health food stores offer the natural foods, fruits and vegetables grown in enriched soil which come closest to providing our bodies with the complete nourishment they must have to maintain health and ward off disease some of them now carry.

CHAPTER SIX

FAREWELL TO HUNZA

As THE impending monsoon rains threatened to prevent my return over the passes, my stay in Hunza had to be terminated.

At the end of my last strenuous day, I returned to the comfortable guest chalet to enjoy a short rest before the dinner hour at the palace. My manservant served hot tea and fresh fruits in the sitting room, and after a refreshing bath and change of clothes I presented myself on the palace balcony. The Mir and his royal household customarily enjoy an hour or so of conversation before the evening meal, and I was delighted to be included.

HUNZA LAND

The Mir's travels take him away from Hunza for considerable periods of time and, of course, he is then unable to follow his regular Hunza customs. As a result, he thoughtfully feels that visitors should be accorded the type of food and drink they are accustomed to, and he imports many delicacies for that purpose. When he asked me if I wished something before dinner, he casually mentioned French champagnes, rare Italian wines, Scotch whisky, Russian vodka and several other appropriate choices. However, I loyally maintained my preference for Hunza Pani, cautioning that I wanted a *small* portion.

Of course, the children were present, although they ate in their own dining room, and it was a pleasure to see how well-mannered they were and how handsome they looked in their native costumes. Their eyes sparkled as they gathered in a semicircle at my feet and asked for "another story." "The Three Bears" interested them, and they animatedly acted out the parts as I spoke. The Crown Prince Ghazanfar was fascinated with the few simple magic tricks I was able to perform.

FAREWELL TO HUNZA

Dinner, as usual, was served in impeccable style, with beautiful shining silver and priceless china making the table a delightful picture. A manservant stood behind each diner and anticipated every need. One of the appealing dishes served was Hunza Kalochees—spiced meat wrapped in *chappati* dough and deep-fried in apricot-seed oil. As the Hunzukuts never eat pies or cakes, dessert consisted of fruit sauce thickened with gelatin. After dinner tea was served in the living room.

The Mir and his brother were in a jovial mood, and I was introduced to the kindly type of humor characteristic of Hunza jokes. Apparently, no pressing affairs of state cast a shadow on the evening, and everything was informal and unhurried.

The Mir spoke of a possible duck- and goose-hunting jaunt to one of Hunza's large lakes. Generally, up to one hundred fowl are shot in a day, each retrieved by a man as there are no hunting dogs in Hunza. Snow leopard, Polo sheep and ibex hunting offer good sport, too, and the Mir planned to take advantage of it later in the season.

His Highness talked at length about the United

States. He assured me he was gratified by Art Linkletter's interest in Hunza, and he recounted some of the stories he had heard of Art's kindness and generosity.

As usual, the Rani was quiet and gracious as she poured tea and acted the perfect hostess. I regretted that Her Highness' unfamiliarity with English prevented her from taking an active part in the conversation, but I am sure she picked up quite a little of what was said.

On this final evening, the customary exchange of gifts was in order. For my wife there was an elaborate tapestry of beautiful embroidery work, which must have taken months or years of painstaking stitching. It was predominantly blue, with colored birds, flowers and arabesques joined in marvelous symmetry and harmony. I recalled seeing a similar tapestry in the palace of the Mir.

The Rani gave my wife an exquisitely colored and stitched pillbox hat. I was the proud recipient of a Hunza coat and a cap to match. This *choga* was made of rich brown homespun cloth from

FAREWELL TO HUNZA

Hunza sheep, and the detailed embroidery work was in red silk.

As we were sitting in the palace living room, a manservant—to my surprise—placed my sun helmet on an end table next to the Mir's chair. The Mir picked up the helmet and said, "I would feel highly honored if I could autograph this, Dr. Banik, and wish you a safe journey." The Mir's suggestion was enthusiastically seconded by the Rani and all the children. The Rani wrote in Urdu: "Dr. Banik is a very kind man—Rani of Hunza." The children followed in order, drawing pictures and writing their messages of good luck. I had expected to discard this helmet in Pakistan, but now it became a cherished possession. Today, covered in protective transparent plastic, it hangs in a prominent place behind my desk—a constant reminder of Hunza and my warm feeling for the Mir and his wonderful family.

We gave our hearts as we distributed the gifts. And, to me was given the greatest honor a Hunza ruler can bestow upon a guest. I was proclaimed a member of the family, an honor granted only to two persons; it is the highest distinction that can be awarded. Tears filled my eyes as I felt the full import of the Mir's regard.

At ten o'clock, much later than the Mir's usual hour of retiring, I returned to the guest chalet and stood silently for a few minutes to etch on my memory the indescribable scene of the Hunza valley in the bright moonlight.

The ageless mountains, dominated by the shimmering grandeur of ice-capped Mt. Rakaposhi, seemed to be sentinels guarding the little kingdom from the turmoil and strife of the outside world. The terraced fields, climbing toward the high cliffs, were dappled patterns of moonlight and shadow, and the whitewashed houses silently held the secret of happy home life perpetuated through the centuries. This was Hunza—a softly brushed picture of peace and God's grandeur.

Early the next morning, we were ready to set forth on the arduous journey across the mountains. The Mir had very kindly placed his best jeep and

FAREWELL TO HUNZA

most experienced driver at my disposal. This vehicle, used often by His Highness, was equipped with a top, a welcome relief from the beating sun.

After a bounteous breakfast, the Mir and Prince Ayash accompanied me to the waiting jeep. A group of natives was on hand to watch our departure, among them the little boy who had loyally followed me as I went about the town. I was glad to see my tiny "Sinbad," and I felt sure he would someday be starting out on a trip of adventure of his own. He had a look in his eyes that seemed to reach beyond horizons.

The jeep engine coughed into action, and as the wheels began to roll, the Mir's parting words were: "I have telephoned ahead, and my men are alerted. They will help you through the washouts. If God is willing, we will see you in America!"

As we moved away, I caught a glimpse of the Rani on the balcony waving her handkerchief.

"Nice people, nice time," cameraman Mahmood said as we made a turn that cut the palace from our view. How aptly these brief words summed up my own feelings! The Mir and his charming family, the friendly people of Hunza, the beautiful little valley kingdom . . . all had become dear to my heart.

Glancing around to see if my baggage was in place, I spied little "Sinbad" jackknifed on a suitcase, grinning hopefully at me.

"Hey, you rascal, come down!" I smiled, pointing to my lap.

He nimbly climbed to his seat of honor, and I couldn't resist squeezing him and wishing he were mine to take along.

"Just how far is he planning to go?" I asked the driver.

"He go about five miles; then he run back."

"Won't his parents worry?"

"Oh, no, he good boy. He come back. No worry."

That relieved my mind, so I gave my attention to watching him wave to his little friends along the way. He was the "littlest big shot" in Hunza!

As we neared the five-mile point, the boy began to feel uneasy, so we stopped to let him off. I

FAREWELL TO HUNZA

gave "Sinbad" a parting pat on the shoulder and a handful of Pakistan money, and he waved wistfully at us until we disappeared around a jutting cliff.

It was early, and the air was still chilly as the sun began tinting the snow-capped peaks around us. The jeep purred along under the guidance of the expert driver. This time, the brakes were good, and I was able to get more relaxed enjoyment of the beauty of the rugged scenery. When the road was too hazardous or the climb too steep, we dismounted and made our way on foot while the driver skilfully took the vehicle past the bad spots.

Often there were just inches between the hub caps and a towering wall, with a dizzy chasm on the opposite side. In places, considerable speed was needed to lend impetus for a sharp rise, and I broke out in a cold sweat in remembrance of the previous trip along this route with the wild-eyed driver who seemed to care so little for life.

Rounding a sharp turn, we suddenly saw a huge cloud high up on the mountainside.

"Look! A fire!" I shouted.

But the driver shook his head, muttering, "Rock-slide. Coming our way."

I was terrified at the thought of being hurled into the canyon or buried alive on the ledge.

The driver glanced upward quickly, then shifted into second gear and stepped on the accelerator. The road wasn't too rough here, and with sufficient speed we might make it.

Instinctively I covered my head with my arms, as the sound of the slide became a roar. We reached the other side just as an avalanche of huge boulders covered the road, not a hundred yards behind us, and hurtled into the abyss. This might be everyday work to native trail men, but I scarcely dared to look at what would have been our fate! And, too, I did not forget that we would have been delayed for hours if the driver had not taken that calculated risk.

The radiator was boiling, and a rushing mountain stream furnished needed water, while we removed our shoes and socks and cooled our burning feet. After fifteen minutes, we hurried on in order

FAREWELL TO HUNZA

to pass two washout spots before the noonday sun melted the snows and sent torrents of water down from the mountains. We saw several of the Mir's men along the trail, but fortunately we did not need their services.

The steep descent, seeming almost vertical to me at some places, took us down to the approach of the shaky bridge that spanned the Hunza river. The noise was deafening, but the icy water had cooled the air, giving us an interval of blessed relief from the 115-degree heat. We crossed the bridge on foot this time, clinging apprehensively to the low handrails.

As we reached the end of the bridge, I turned to take a last look at Hunza and saw the tip of majestic Mt. Rakaposhi far in the distance. I blew a farewell kiss to the famed peak as we headed for Chalt, where we were to have lunch and then proceed to Gilgit, the northernmost airstrip in Pakistan.

I had expected the trip into Gilgit to be uneventful, and had mentally relaxed in the belief that the strenuous physical effort of my adventure had

HUNZA LAND

been completed. However, to my dismay, we were held up by two washouts. Here was real physical effort again. It took us two hours to fill in the first wash sufficiently to cross; the second took somewhat less time, but I was pretty well exhausted. (Too bad the Mir's stalwarts could not have helped us on this stretch of road. However, we were no longer in Hunza.) The wind had become appreciably hotter, and we suffered more because we were traveling with it. It was ideal sunstroke weather.

After a grueling, eight-hour ride, we finally reached the Gilgit River not far from the town of the same name. One more river crossing, and then it would be planes all the way.

As we descended the final pass into the valley, I noticed some forbidding low clouds on the horizon. The monsoons were about to start! If I couldn't get out of Gilgit quickly, it would mean a six-week stayover. Everything would be fine if I could just reach Rawalpindi because the large planes were not grounded by the rains, and the country was flat.

Reaching Gilgit, we sought at once the hospitality

FAREWELL TO HUNZA

of the Northern Scout lodge where I had stayed before. We arrived just in time for dinner, and my dusty baggage was taken to the same small room where I had been quartered before. It was a pleasure to rejoin the friendly men around the dining table, and they expressed keen interest in my Hunza visit.

The English of these men was limited and short expressions made up the conversation. "Bad roads, big mountains, Hunza far away, bad rockslides, not me go there, etc.," were typical. I found myself conversing in words rather than sentences. It is surprising how much information can be exchanged in that way.

When I asked about the plane schedule for the return trip, I was struck speechless when I learned that the plane was out of service because of serious engine trouble. Nobody knew when it would be repaired; parts were almost impossible to get in that remote region. I did manage to ask, "How soon will the rains start?"

The answer was, "Never know exact time. Overhanging clouds [those I had seen] a sure sign."

HUNZA LAND

This was bad news. A six-week delay in Gilgit was unthinkable. For one thing, if my films could not be processed quickly they would be ruined. Temperatures were excessive and there was, of course, no refrigeration.

I slept very little that night. As there was no road to Rawalpindi, Pakistan, any thought of going by jeep was eliminated. The Mir had told me of making this trip by horseback, but, as my experience with horses was limited to watching TV westerns, this was no solution for me. Clouds were moving sullenly over the morning sky and the feel of the sultry air further depressed my spirits. Low clouds, of course, would prevent any flight between the narrow openings through the mountains.

I walked gloomily into the dining room of the lodge and found four uniformed men I had not seen before. They introduced themselves, in fluent English, as Pakistanian army fliers, and they were the jolliest, most talkative group of men I had seen in a long time. The Captain, I learned, was

FAREWELL TO HUNZA

the instructor of the three others, who were student fliers.

"You are fliers?" I almost shouted. "You have a plane?"

The bearded, impeccably uniformed Captain laughed. "Why, of course. We flew up here to evacuate some of our men before the monsoon rains set in."

When I excitedly asked if he would take two civilian passengers, he shrugged, and said, "I am very sorry, sir, but army regulations forbid that."

In spite of this refusal, I told the officer of my predicament and explained why I had to reach Rawalpindi before the rains. My references to television fascinated him; he had a real desire to appear on TV, and he longed to visit the United States.

As I wanted to enlist the support of these men in getting me a lift to Rawalpindi, I said, "I should like to take some pictures of you men. You are the happiest group of fliers I have ever seen, and I want to have pictures to remember you by." The men were very glad to oblige, and from the way they posed for the photographs I am sure they all had a little ham-actor blood in their veins.

All the time I was shooting the pictures, I sought some solution to the problem of getting on that plane. Finally, I said, "By the way, Captain, would it be possible for me to go along if I signed a paper releasing your government from liability? If an accident should happen, no action could be taken. That is all the protection they need." I could tell by the Captain's expression that the idea seemed to have possibilities, and I was sure he wanted to help me.

As he considered the suggestion, an officer of the Political Agents Department of Affairs stepped into the room. I had talked to him before, of course, but I now explained my position again and advanced the suggestion I had made to the Captain.

After a few moments' hesitation, he replied: "I think it could be arranged, Captain. If I write up the papers and you both sign, I see no reason why the doctor couldn't fly with you."

"May I sign the papers as quickly as possible?" I asked. "We have less than an hour before takeoff."

FAREWELL TO HUNZA

The Department officer located some carbon paper, and typed an original and several copies of the liability release. With each click of the machine, I found myself closer to my stowaway air passage. At last it was finished. Without stopping to read it carefully, I signed.

"We will fly in thirty minutes," the Captain said. "Please have your baggage at the plane as soon as possible."

As I rushed to get my equipment together, I stopped short and looked at my watch. It was ten-thirty. Where was Mahmood? He had spent the night in the village, but had been told to report at ten this morning. He had never been late before.

"Mahmood, where are you? We are leaving!" I shouted at nobody as I rushed to the road on the hill. Not a soul was about, but suddenly I heard a jeep grinding down a steep hill in low gear. If I could commandeer that jeep, perhaps I could locate him! Finally, the dilapidated vehicle crawled into view, and there was my cameraman sitting in back, in perfect ease, smoking a big cigar.

"Mahmood, we're leaving! Where have you

been? The plane is waiting for us!" I cried.

He calmly replied, "No plane. Plane broke down. No hurry."

I convinced him that we really were going, and our respective baggage was quickly rounded up.

I caught my breath as I looked at the plane. It was an old "box car" that should have been scrapped twenty years before! The paint was entirely gone; the belly was caved in; the four-bladed propellers looked uneven.

"Will it really fly?" I asked the Captain.

"Of course, Doctor. It does need a little repairing and we will be considerably overloaded, but we'll make it—with God's help."

This is the philosophy of the people of Pakistan; take what you have and try to make it do, always hoping for a better day. For me this battered ship had to do; there was no other way to get to Rawalpindi.

It was time to go aboard, and I hoped for some relief inside from the almost unbearable 118-degree temperature. To my dismay, it was even hotter under the uninsulated metal. There were benches

FAREWELL TO HUNZA

along the sides of the cabin, with a wire strung overhead for use by paratroops. Chutes were piled carelessly in one heap, and all the baggage was jumbled in another.

The veteran engines were warmed up, and we rumbled down the bumpy runway with the mountains staring at us only a short distance ahead. The plane raised one wing and then the other, as the framework creaked and groaned. Airspeed was not sufficient to clear the mountain on the first try, so the Captain made a U-turn and gained enough altitude on the second run to top the barrier by seeming inches.

Then started a never-to-be-forgotten zigzagging —dodging one wall after another with the wings almost touching the rocks. Mahmood tried to take some pictures through the porthole, but the lurching and the dust-crusted glass made him abandon the effort.

Finally the wheels touched down on the Rawalpindi airport, and rolled nearly to the end of the long strip, as braking power was negligible. I heaved a deep sigh and peered through the grimy window. It was raining; we had beaten the deluge by minutes!

As we stepped from the plane, Major Hasam greeted me with a big smile and a hearty handshake.

"You made a very fortunate landing, Doctor," he said. "A half hour from now, it would be difficult. You must have a lucky emblem with you. But we need these monsoons, for our fields are parched and our cattle are starving. It will be better now."

I said a regretful goodbye to Mahmood, who had done such a wonderful job of photography for me. He was a good companion and a true friend. Then I joined the Captain and his charges in the officers' room for a cup of tea. I can't recall when I have accepted an invitation so heartily. The Captain had done me a tremendous favor, and he was a master pilot. The companionship of his group was a tonic for the spirit.

The rain came down in torrents as the Major's car carried me toward the familiar hotel where I had stayed before. All my friends were there—the Brevaires, the Hollingsworths, and many, many more. American-like, they were ready for refresh-

FAREWELL TO HUNZA

ments, and for a detailed account of my experiences in Hunza. The women, of course, clamored to see the gifts I had brought back from the fabled valley. There were shrieks of delight as I proudly displayed the beautifully worked tapestry, the gorgeous silks, the ibex wools and the Hunza coats and caps. The apparel was modeled noisily by the ladies—and attractively, too, I might add.

When the chatter had subsided a little, I announced that I had still another proof that I had been in Hunza. I left the room and returned in a moment with a cloth-wrapped package, which I began to unwrap slowly.

"This, my friends, is a bottle of the famous Hunza Water—that makes the people of Hunza happy!" I said as I held the bottle aloft.

Art Brevaire leaped forward and I handed him the bottle to examine. He grasped it firmly and held it close as he stepped back with arm raised in an exaggerated protective gesture. I laughingly protested that the bottle was to be given to the Dunker's Club at the Fort Kearney Hotel. I explained that Jim Boyd, one of our members, hadn't been moving around too spryly and I had hoped this tonic might be beneficial.

Not intimidated in the least, Art assured me loudly, "You're not going to take this Hunza Water to that coffee club in Kearney, Nebraska! You promised to pay us off when you got back, and this is the payoff. Tell that coffee club they can drink tea!"

The chant went up "We want Hunza Water! We want Hunza Water!" They got it. The effect was as advertised.

The following day was spent in saying good-bye to the many Pakistanian officials and to the Americans who had befriended and assisted me. Commander Maqbool and Major Hasam and his staff were gratified at my successful trip, and they were happy that their Department of Public Relations had helped. I thanked them all warmly.

It was time to pick up my plane ticket for Karachi. The same pretty clerk who arranged for my charter passage to Gilgit was behind the desk in the airline office. Miss Shahida Ahmad, a British university graduate, had previously helped me

FAREWELL TO HUNZA

through some translation difficulties and I wanted to add her photo to the picture record of my trip.

When I asked for permission to take the photo, the lady said, "Doctor, will you send me one?"

When I assured her I would do so, she countered, "Oh, you Americans are all the same; you promise to send a picture, but never do!"

I decided to give her a surprise this time, so I snapped the shot with the Polaroid Land Camera I happened to have with me. In just one minute after the shutter clicked, I handed her a perfect picture of herself. She was so amazed that she had to sit down; it was her first experience with this remarkable camera. I remember taking a picture of an old man in Gilgit. He had never seen his likeness in a mirror and he did not recognize his own face in the picture. Perhaps I shouldn't have disillusioned him!

Next stop was Karachi and here I spent a brief time in jail! It seems I had neglected to report my arrival in Rawalpindi to the police of that city and a jail sentence was the possible result. However, an understanding official quickly had me released, after the necessary papers were signed. The Pakistanians are very wise to keep an observant eye on foreign visitors, and I regretted that I had not complied with their laws.

As I stepped into the Dutch Airlines Constellation on the Karachi field, I seemed to turn over a page in my life; the final page in a too short chapter that enabled me to live, briefly, an experience I had dreamed of for twenty years.

CHAPTER SEVEN

THE HUNZA LESSON

HEADING west again—this time over the Atlantic toward home—I mentally turned back toward Hunza. I thought of the Mir and his attractive family; the rugged beauty of the countryside with its soil-rich little fields climbing far up the mountains; the white-capped grandeur of Mt. Rakaposhi.

In Hunza, I seemed to be in another world; a world of friendliness and good nature. Covetousness, envy and jealousy were nonexistent; no police force was needed to keep order; unlocked doors were not a temptation. But I was most strongly impressed by the evidences of good health I witnessed among the Hunzukuts of all ages. Their freedom from a variety of diseases and physical ailments was remarkable. Cancer, heart attacks, vascular complaints and many of the common childhood diseases such as mumps, measles and chicken pox are unknown among them.

I am convinced that the diet upon which these people have lived for centuries is responsible for the enviable good health they enjoy. It cannot be matched in our civilization with its depleted soils, processed foods robbed of life-giving elements, and cooking methods that effectively destroy a substantial percentage of the vitamins and trace elements that are essential to sound bodies. The example of the Hunzukuts in agriculture and eating habits can be profitably followed in the United States, which leads the world in material progress and standards of good living. Yet, in respect to the raising of truly nutritious food, it lags far behind the little kingdom of Hunza.

What I learned there centered my attention on the subjects of nutrition and soil. Of course, I had previously been aware of the basic facts of nutrition and the value of a balanced diet. However, like

THE HUNZA LESSON

many others, I ate what was served to me, not questioning the nutritive value of the food, where it came from or whether or not my body required it.

My attitude toward eating changed radically after I observed the Hunza way of life. I realized that it is time for the Western world to awaken to facts and do something about changing its "civilized" habits.

Increasing efforts to use the soil properly in the production of health-building foodstuffs are already being made in various sections of our country. The gratifying patronage enjoyed by growers who raise truly nutritious vegetables and fruits on properly enriched soil make me confident that the future holds promise. As this kind of organic farming is expanded, thousands more men, women and children will begin to enjoy the radiant health that only natural foods can provide.

Eventually, a large segment of our population—those who are alert to the importance of good nutrition—will be able to procure the naturally grown foods that are essential in building strong bodies.

Natural food supplements are helping significantly in making it possible right now to obtain the balanced nourishment our bodies need.

In a talk to members of the American Medical Association (reported in *Newsweek,* June 17, 1959), Tom Douglas Spies, M.D., a recipient of the A.M.A. Distinguished Service Award, said: "All disease is caused by chemicals, and all disease can be cured by chemicals. All the chemicals used by the body, except for the oxygen we breathe and the water we drink, are taken in through food. If we only knew enough, all disease could be prevented and could be cured through proper nutrition."

Are the people of Hunza a confirmation of Dr. Spies's theory? Perhaps, by their two thousand years' isolation from "advanced" methods the Hunzukuts have unwittingly preserved a regimen which can teach us a lesson in better general health. I am willing to believe this after my experience in their beautiful valley.

How can we take the fullest advantage of the

THE HUNZA LESSON

"Hunza lesson" in nutrition? We can do so by paying attention to the following regime:

1. Buy organically grown garden vegetables and fruit either direct from the grower or from a grocer who purchases his produce daily from a nearby grower.
2. Buy fresh produce only in such quantity as can be consumed soon. There is value to freshness.
3. Always select choice looking vegetables and fruit. It is false economy to buy less than the best.
4. Never skin or peel vegetables; the skin contains a great part of the nutrients.
5. Steam or cook vegetables in as small a quantity of water as possible and do not overcook. Use the juices and water.
6. Eat liberal portions of salads and raw root vegetables twice daily.
7. Keep fresh fruits available in season.
8. Substitute dried fruits (preferably sun-dried and unsulphured) when fresh fruits are not available. Use the water in which they are soaked or cooked.

9. Eat germinated grain or beans, especially in winter and early spring.
10. Include animal organs (brain, kidney, liver, etc.) if meat is used.
11. Insist on whole-meal bread; stone-ground if procurable.
12. Eat fresh-churned butter and unprocessed cheese.
13. Drink milk, buttermilk, skimmed milk or yogurt.
14. Confine number of foods eaten at one meal to a palatable minimum.
15. Whole-grain cereals and seed cereals, such as millet.*
16. Apricot oil, sunflower oil, sesame oil.†
17. Sunflower seeds.‡
18. Herb teas.

Most of us think of nutrition as something that provides the body with food. This is true, but to understand the essentials of good nutrition we must

---

* Millet is rich in protein.
† Recommended for salads as well as for cooking.
‡ A remarkably rich source of minerals and vitamins.

THE HUNZA LESSON

realize that the body—bone, muscle, skin, glands and nerves—is composed of cells. Each of these billions of cells has a specific job to do, and it must have the proper nutrients if it is to do the job effectively. It is easier to appreciate the necessity for proper nutrition when the requirements of the cells are considered.

As the cells wear out they are replaced by others and, if proper nourishment is provided, the new cells retain the healthy qualities of the old. Thus proper diet can prevent cell starvation which, scientists claim, is the early stage of aging.

The bodies of many people start to deteriorate in middle life because their diets lack protein, vitamins and minerals. The importance of protein cannot be overemphasized. Without it the essential enzymes and hormones cannot be produced properly, wastes collect in the tissues, blood fails to clot, and antibodies that fight virus and toxic invaders are not manufactured in adequate quantities. Continued protein deficiency causes the skin to dry up and wrinkle, and premature old age is the result.

The essential substance of living cells is protoplasm, the physical basis of all organic life. Protoplasm is a viscous (gluey) material made up of hydrogen and oxygen (water), nitrogen, carbon and several other elements in varied combinations. The nitrogenous substances (proteins) are important in protoplasm structure, and so are inorganic salts and lecithin (phosphorized fat). The latter facilitates absorption of nutrient, the discharge of the products the cell contributes to body processes, and the elimination of the end-products of chemical activities.

The directing center of the activity of the cell is the nucleus. This is a network of filaments, the meshes of which are filled with a protein containing phosphorus (nucleo-protein). Along the filaments are granules of an iron-containing protein (chromatin). All vital processes depend on the completeness of the nucleus and sound structure of its proteins.

The composition of a person's body depends on what he eats. Food from vegetable and animal sources consists mainly of matter that is living or formerly living. Living tissues of the body cannot be sustained from food which has, or has had, no

THE HUNZA LESSON

life. Plants, for example, transmute inorganic substances—water, carbon dioxide, mineral salts—from the earth and air into organic food which is either eaten as plants or as animals which have been nourished on organic food. Man is created out of the earth.

Food is anything which, when digested, furnishes the materials that the cells need to keep their structure healthy and their functions normal. The essential materials are oxygen, water, carbohydrates, proteins, vitamins and inorganic elements.

In addition to oxygen and water, there are twenty-nine known indispensables: ten amino-acids (derived from food proteins); eleven inorganic elements (calcium, sodium, iron, magnesium, phosphorus, potassium, sulphur, copper, manganese, iodine, chlorine); linoleic acid (from fats).

No single food provides all these essentials; therefore, a properly balanced diet should be sought—a combination of foods that will supply all of the essentials in proper quantity and balance. The latter is important, because the lack or inadequacy of one essential can spoil the effectiveness of the whole diet.

HUNZA LAND

The quality of food is, of course, an important consideration. Cultivation methods play an important part in providing body-building essentials. Hunza gardens and fields grow exceptionally nourishing produce because all the organic elements taken from the soil by crops are returned to the soil, and rich minerals are provided in the silt from the mountain water which is used for irrigation.

Examples of disease resulting from inadequate diet among human beings in different countries, and in various sections of the same country, are too numerous to mention; beri-beri, pellagra, goiter and rickets are but a few. When proper diet is instituted, the diseases disappear.

Proof of the relationship of diet to disease is dramatically illustrated by the fact that many specific diseases can be produced in experimental animals by changing the components of their diets. Good health cannot be enjoyed if all cells and organs of the body are not functioning properly; and they cannot function properly if they do not receive the required nourishment.

The most essential things necessary for adequate

THE HUNZA LESSON

nourishment of the human body and for physical well-being are present in whole-cereal grains, root and leafy vegetables, legumes, fruits, and milk and milk products, with an occasional egg or serving of meat.

Of course, a diet must be complete. Substitution of whole-meal bread for white bread, for instance, will be of no benefit if the change does not completely restore the balance of an ill-balanced diet. What should be realized is that foods mentioned above will maintain body efficiency if eaten in adequate quantities.

I am sure the Hunzukuts do not realize their bodies are so complicated, and I doubt that many of us give the matter any thought. However, it deserves serious thought to realize that the absence of one or more of these materials may make you feel below par, or actually cause illness.

It is common knowledge that a deficiency of iron in the diet causes anemia. But, the medical profession generally agrees, a deficiency of copper or cobalt also will cause anemia. Insufficient iodine over a period of time can lead to goiter. Active body tissue deteriorates if phosphorus is lacking; nervous disorders result from magnesium deficiency, and so on.

We are told that the logical way to keep the body supplied with essential components is through customary diet. I have seen with my own eyes how well the diet of the Hunzukuts seems to replenish the necessary elements in their systems. But how do *we* come out on body replenishment?

People pay little attention to their health until they lose it; then they suddenly become awake and try to buy it back at any price. Health cannot be bought with money. We have to use our common sense and make it a daily practice to eat properly and sensibly.

We must meet the daily food intake requirements and, to do that, we must know the fundamental facts; we cannot leave it to chance. Even though we eat more than the recommended quantity of foods on a "health diet," we are still lacking in necessary minerals and vitamins if the soil is not fertile. In this case it is absolutely essential to add

THE HUNZA LESSON

a well-balanced intake of natural minerals, vitamins and proteins.

There is a tremendous variation in the composition of grain, vegetables, fruit, meat, eggs and milk in different parts of the country and even on different fields on the same farm. It is significant, I think, that such variations are not found on the farms in the Hunza valley.

A good many of us believe—and I must confess I used to be among them—that the minute quantities of elements needed by our bodies do not have much effect on health. For nearly two hundred years we have eaten the foods produced on our farm soils, and have enjoyed a fairly good state of health. However, the striking increase in degenerative diseases of the heart, teeth, bones and liver should make us take a second look at how well our soils are providing the nutritive elements we need.

When our country was first settled, the soils were virgin. They contained adequate quantities of the minerals required for human health. Many minerals came from the waters of the sea. Dead animals and birds were left on the soil to return to it the elements they had received from it. Vegetation died and returned again to the soil. This process of building soil fertility, of course, approximates the agricultural methods of the Hunzukuts, who return to the soil everything—animal and vegetable —that comes from the soil originally.

But what has happened to our soils to make them produce diseased and insect-ridden plants and unhealthy animals? For generations, the crops and livestock grown on our soils have been shipped to the cities. Each year, essential elements have been taken away, not to be returned through natural methods. In a century or two, the once virgin soils became depleted. Erosion and leaching aided the process. The minerals shipped to the cities were wasted as sewage or in garbage dumps and incinerators.

A dramatic example of how valuable minerals are lost in city sewage is provided by experiments conducted by Carl Chin, an Omaha, Nebraska, chemist. According to an article appearing in the *Omaha World Herald,* July 22, 1959, Mr. Chin is

THE HUNZA LESSON

growing huge vegetables in his garden plot, using sludge from the Omaha sewage treatment plant to enrich the soil. Melons "large enough to hold a duck" and string beans eighteen inches long are but two of the varieties of succulent vegetables he has produced. The chemist states that the activated sludge is more a soil conditioner than a fertilizer. It adds humus, permitting moisture absorption, and it prevents the soil from packing down. There is a lesson here for many of our vegetable and fruit growers.

Of course, some effort is now being made to replenish the soil by use of commercial fertilizers which contain some of the needed elements. However, not all of the elements are restored, and deficiencies in diets inevitably result.

Sir Robert McCarrison, the author of *Nutrition and Health,* in his exhaustive diet experiments with white rats proved conclusively that diets which cause deficiency diseases in human beings also produce similar diseases in the rats. Diets on which human beings enjoy robust health also keep rats in comparable good health. In reviewing the results of these experiments, I was not at all surprised to find that foods grown by the people of Hunza maintained the rats in exceptionally good health.

The body's daily requirements for many vitamins and minerals have been established, but there are others known to be necessary to keep up perfect health, although definite requirements have not been determined. Deficiency of any may lead to a run-down condition, and possibly serious illness.

A balanced, natural diet should supply us with all the proteins, vitamins and minerals our bodies need. Yet, even though greater quantities of the specified foods are eaten than are recommended, serious deficiencies exist among our population.

Why is this true? The Hunzukuts do not take bottled vitamins and minerals; indeed, they have never heard of these body essentials. Before the first crops are harvested, their supply of food is drastically limited. However, the food they eat is naturally rich in nutrients and it is consumed, for the most part, in an uncooked state.

Cooking reduces the nutritional value of food because it tends to destroy certain amino-acids, par-

THE HUNZA LESSON

ticularly lysine, which is the most important of the entire group of protein components. Lysine raises (from 50 to 100 per cent) the ability of bread and cereal to build and repair muscle and organ tissue. It improves the appetite; markedly increases resistance to infection; often raises the hemoglobin level where iron therapy fails; and proves dramatically helpful in restoring and maintaining the health of elderly people. The body's inability to manufacture lysine makes it imperative to add this lifegiving "building block" to diets insufficient in it. Otherwise from 25 to 40 per cent of protein intake fails to nourish adequately. Protein deficiency is a primary world health problem today. Low energy and a "dragged out" feeling are symptoms.

Pasteurization and cooking destroy enzymes—the substances that speed chemical changes in the body. The importance of the enzymes in connection with diet is suggested by the fact that nourishment from food cannot enter the blood stream until it has been conditioned by autolysis through enzymic action.

If we eat more than is necessary, and still show

signs of deficiencies, it is obvious that our foods do not contain the essential elements the body needs. Someone coined this phrase: "Starving to death on a full stomach."

Not only are our grains, vegetables and fruits lacking in food values when they are harvested or gathered, but they lose more of such protein-vitamin-mineral values in transportation and storage. Then "processing" takes away still more. Add to this the additional loss as a result of improper cooking methods, and you can see why something must be done to assure our population of adequate nourishment.

Of course, the housewife can make an intelligent selection of the foods that will help promote the well-being of her family; and, she can do such cooking as is necessary in a way that will preserve the natural goodness and values of the food. Refined grain products (flour), refined sugar, polished rice and processed fruits should, as a rule, be omitted from the diet.

Organically rich foods are so superior that, once they are tried, the "old diet" will seem insipid and

THE HUNZA LESSON

unattractive. I shall never forget the natural sweetness and marvelous taste of the fruits and vegetables I enjoyed in Hunza!

Most of us completely fail to understand the importance of a balanced mineral supply in building and maintaining robust health. Many people can glibly recite the virtues of some of the vitamins they take regularly, but overlook the fact that without minerals the vitamins are useless. Balanced nutrition demands that enough of all the essential minerals be present to perform their duties as body rebuilders and to work harmoniously with the vitamins.

Our education on vitamins is much broader than it is on minerals, and the general knowledge of this dietary need is all to the good. All humans are vulnerable to disease and infection no matter how "healthy" they may appear to be, and the ability to fight off these ills depends on the body resistance that is built up by a balanced supply of vitamins, minerals and proteins.

To date, nearly thirty minerals have been recognized as necessary to good health. As mineral salts, they are regulators and builders of the cells which make up the body. Strong bones, firm muscles, an alert mind, sound teeth, steady nerves and healthy organs require these minerals in adequate quantity. Vitamins cannot accomplish their purpose without minerals; this is why balanced nutrition is imperative. When we get nervous and irritable, we do not realize that lack of calcium may be responsible. If we have good teeth, we do not credit the phosphorus and calcium that made them possible.

Calcium. It is generally agreed that a person needs about four grams of calcium per day, yet less than one gram is usually taken into the body in the usual diet. Probably calcium is the mineral in which we are most deficient, and the lack is evidenced by excessive tooth decay, taut nerves, flabby muscles, and bones that break easily.

Nervousness, cramps, and rapid heartbeat are indications of calcium deficiency. Fresh fruits and vegetables, whole grains, nuts and sprouts provide calcium in good quantity, and some of the specific foods that are rich in this mineral are listed here, together with their calcium contents:

The Mir of Hunza's palace.

The Mir of Hunza in royal attire, holding a six-hundred-year-old sword and enjoying the novelty of American sun glasses. His two sons are at the author's left.

A Hunza child with beautiful Mt. Rakaposhi in the background, a majestic sight from the valley.

Hunza terraces, each irrigated by glacier waters through master canals.

The author appears before the Mir's Council of Elders. The Mir, standing at the far right, is wearing his carefully tailored native costume. Mt. Rakaposhi is in the distance.

Friendly Hunza women in native dress.

The author with a group of Hunzakuts whose eyes he has just examined and found nearly perfect. The glasses they wear are complimentary pairs; after the novelty wore off the men removed them.

The author examining a hollowed gourd in which Hunza Water is kept remarkably cool before being served at meals.

THE HUNZA LESSON

FOOD SOURCE	MEASURE	CALCIUM MG.
Almonds	¼ C.	144
Bone meal (veal, raw)	½ C.	305
Cheese, Cheddar	1 inch cube	183
Cheese, Swiss	1 inch cube	244
Collards, raw or cooked	½ C.	250
Kale	½ C.	225
Milk, dry, skim	¼ C.	310
Milk, dry-fed	8 oz.	275
Milk, goat's	8 oz.	305
Molasses, blackstrap	1 T.	116
Molasses, dark	1 T.	58
Soybean flour	1 C.	330

To accomplish its purpose, calcium must be properly absorbed. The hydrochloric acid in the stomach is the agent which combines with this mineral to hold it in solution for absorption in the small intestines. Inadequate stomach acid allows calcium to remain insoluble, and it is then lost through elimination. This chemistry illustrates how important it is to have normally functioning organs. Everything in the body is interdependent, and we can get the full benefit of minerals and vitamins only when the "team" is working efficiently as a whole.

Phosphorus. Phosphorus is an important hardening agent of the bones and teeth, and is found in the structure of each cell nucleus. This mineral acts to maintain acid-alkaline balance in the blood and urine; it aids muscles to contract; and it is absolutely necessary in milk formation. Phosphorous activates enzymes and assists in the breakdown of carbohydrates and fats.

The absorption process of phosphorus is the same as that of calcium. If there is not enough calcium to combine with it, the phosphorus is evacuated through the kidneys. Phosphorus deficiency leads to poor bone formation, abnormal teeth, rickets, poor appetite, weight loss and body weakness.

Protein-rich foods that contain phosphorus in quantity are wheat, oats, rye, cheese, milk, eggs, meats, beans, peas, legumes, soybeans, nuts. Nearly all fruits and vegetables contain some phosphorus.

Iron. Iron is the mineral that builds the red blood cells which bring oxygen to all the cells of the body and takes away carbon-dioxide. The red cells

THE HUNZA LESSON

are "manufacturers" in the marrow of the long bones. They carry hemoglobin, which has an affinity for iron. Red cells are thick and bright red when the diet is rich in iron. If there is an iron deficiency, the red blood cells will be pale in color and thin.

This condition is known as anemia, and a person suffering from it lacks vitality. He is always tired because not enough oxygen reaches the body cells to free them from wastes.

Statistics show that almost 90 per cent of the women in the United States are anemic or bordering on anemia. The condition cannot be determined by a person's weight, age, or size. Often overweight women are anemic, but they lose weight when proper iron intake is instituted.

It is regrettable that such a large proportion of our population suffers from some degree of anemia, because a blood count can determine the condition accurately, and iron administration can bring the blood back to normal. Iron is found in all cells and muscle tissue, and excess is stored in the bone marrow, liver and spleen.

The sources of iron most completely absorbable

HUNZA LAND

are peanuts, blackstrap molasses, and all fresh fruits. Apricots (a main item in the diet of the people of Hunza) are by far the richest source of iron among fruits. The table indicates the importance of apricots.

FOOD SOURCE	MEASURE	IRON MG.
Apricots, dried	5	4.6
Barley, whole	½ C.	5.1
Dates	6—8	2.2
Flour, soybean	1 C.	7.0
Flour, whole wheat	1 C.	4.0
Heart, beef	2 slices	4.6
Liver, beef	2 oz.	5.0
Molasses, blackstrap	1 T.	9.6
Parsley	½ C.	9.6
Raisins	¼ C.	0.9
Wheat germ	½ C.	6.4
Yeast, brewer's	1 T.	2.0

Iodine. The thyroid gland, located at the base of the throat, regulates the metabolism of the body. This gland requires small amounts of iodine to function properly, and lack of this mineral causes a loss in vitality and endurance. Iodine deficiency can produce goiter, accumulation of fat, and even the appearance of stupidity.

Ocean foods, both animal and vegetable, are rich in iodine. Cod liver oil is an excellent source, and dehydrated sea vegetation, such as kelp, offers good concentrations. Iodized salt is regularly used on millions of tables. Plants absorb iodine from the soil, and animals get it from food and water.

However, the soil in many areas is deficient in the mineral, and the plants and animals raised in these localities do not supply enough iodine for the diet. This important mineral is normally present in milk; however, it must be added to the ration of the cows in the areas of deficiency.

It is preferable to get ten to fifty times the amount of iodine required rather than not enough. The mineral is not toxic in food form, and the body discards what is not assimilated.

Copper. Because copper aids the body in the assimilation of iron, its presence in the body is important if anemia is to be avoided. The best food sources for this mineral are whole grains, dried fruits (apricots are especially rich in copper), oysters, clams, liver, molasses, green leaf vegetables, soy flour, and egg yolk.

Sodium. As the blood must be kept neutral (neither acid nor alkaline), a balancing agent is necessary, and sodium fills this important function; it also keeps calcium in solution.

Salt (sodium chloride) is the principal source of sodium for human beings. The mineral is found in vegetables and the muscle of animals. Lack of sodium in the body is most noticeable in hot weather because it is lost in quantity through perspiration. Heat stroke and cramps may result from lack of sodium, and steelworkers and others doing hard manual labor in high temperatures generally take salt tablets to prevent the ill effects of sodium-chloride deficiency.

Potassium. Like sodium, potassium functions as a balancer. The two minerals, in conjunction, attract from the blood stream nourishment that is needed by the body cells. The minerals also assist in ridding the cells of waste.

Potassium is important in body growth, and lack

THE HUNZA LESSON

of it can cause constipation, slow heartbeat, kidney damage and fragile bones.

Blackstrap molasses, leafy green vegetables, whole grains, potatoes, fruits and almonds are excellent sources of potassium.

If you do not want to feel dragged out and weary and wish to postpone wrinkles and other tell-tale signs of the years, it is wise to fortify your diet with a dependable *organic* balanced food supplement. Careful attention should be given to the choice of a supplement to make sure that its sources will provide all the elements necessary to a balanced diet.

Dramatic evidence of the life-sustaining potential of a balanced food supplement is afforded by the experience of Captain DeVere Baker, Redondo Beach, California, shipbuilder and author of the book *The Raft Lehi IV*.* World-wide newspaper accounts of Captain Baker's adventures in drifting from the California coast to Hawaii on the motorless raft tell of the six days the Captain and his three-

* Long Beach, California: Whitehorn Publishing Co., 1959.

man crew spent without food at the conclusion of the sixty-nine day journey.

Although actual food supplies were exhausted after sixty-three days at sea, the men continued taking a food supplement rich in vitamins, minerals and proteins, and also a mineral-rich dehydrated plant of which they made herb tea, doubling the portions taken previously.

Examination by physicians at the end of the voyage proved that all the men were in perfect physical condition, with normal pulse and blood count. Here is an excellent indication of how a balanced food supplement can sustain life and maintain health for a considerable period.

While the importance of good nutrition cannot be overemphasized, there is another factor that contributes to radiant health. Complete elimination is an absolute essential. Constipation, "the father of human diseases," so prevalent in our country, is utterly foreign to the people of Hunza.

This fact seems to suggest that good elimination might be related directly to the simple eating habits of the Hunzukuts and their active way of life. Art

THE HUNZA LESSON

Waerland's book, *In the Cauldron of Disease,* recounts the experience of the famous British surgeon, Sir Arbuthnot Lane, who operated on more than one thousand patients with a variety of diseases. In each instance the colon was removed. Although this organ was not always primarily involved in the complaints, removal of it restored the patients to health.

The subsequent continued good health of these patients led the surgeon to believe that toxins in the colon had caused the trouble. Experiments indicated that refined foods created poisons which were absorbed into the blood stream when wastes remained too long before evacuation.

Further investigations demonstrated that when cellulose was added to the diet it remained in an unchanged state until it passed into the colon. The cellulose did not "pack," and the soft mass permitted the muscles in the colon wall to move it forward easily. Regular eliminations occurred as many times a day as meals were consumed.

From Lane's further studies it was inferred that a fermentation process takes place in the ascending section of the colon and that there is a multiplication of the friendly flora which break down the cellulose and release the trace minerals and other nutrients it contains. These elements, it is believed, are absorbed into the blood stream through the walls of the colon. Thus the organ which had previously been regarded as merely a "storage place" appears as an active part of the digestive system.

As I read Waerland's book I could see that the Hunzukuts' freedom from constipation was obviously due to the abundance of natural cellulose they consumed in their fruits and other foods. This regular elimination of wastes from the body appeared to be a contributing factor to their amazing life span.

Then I came across an article, "The Miracle of Hunza Farm," by Homar Hathaway, in *Ford Farming* magazine, telling about a farm in the northwest, the soil of which has been enriched by natural flooding for untold centuries. A special grass grows in profusion in this beautiful valley. When the present owner bought this farm, ". . . he had but one idea in mind: he wanted a place to hunt. And

THE HUNZA LESSON

the lush valley grass offered ideal protection for duck and pheasant. . . .

"Although several owners had thought the soil there possessed strange qualities, none had thoroughly investigated its possibilities until the present owner bought the land. And even his discovery was a lucky accident. . . .

"When some of his thoroughbred horses began eating the grass he sensed a difference between grass grown here and that grown on neighboring farms. The horses acted almost as if they had been given some kind of pill to pep them up.

"The potential of this excellent grass as a livestock feed gave the owner the idea of dehydrating it and putting it up in large bags to be sold by the ton. Farmers began buying it and some reported amazing results—cows that never dried up, chinchillas whose fur demanded premium prices, dogs whose mange cleared up.

"As the stories traveled, persons afflicted with various diseases began to come around and ask for small samples of the product. Making no claims for the grass, the owner was happy to comply. He

HUNZA LAND

filled any containers they brought free of charge. They wanted to brew a tea with it, they said. But when some of them returned to report amazing developments as to their physical condition he was skeptical. . . .

"Then one day state officials came to Hunza Farm and suggested that he put his product up in boxes. They had no objections to his giving it away but felt he should be more sanitary about it. As an expensive trial, he had 1,000 boxes made up in pound sizes to give away. In two weeks they were gone. . . ."

Analysis of the Hunza Farm grass shows that it contains mineral salts such as sodium, calcium, manganese, nickel, potassium, phosphorus, cobalt, boron, titanium, chromium and several others. The grass also contains coloring matter consisting of chlorophyll,* alpha and beta caretene, menthophyll, anthocyamins, and the enzyme chlorophyllase. This wealth of minerals is accounted for by the fact

---

* Chlorophyll is tremendously important in making blood. It has the same chemical makeup as hemoglobin except that its nucleus is magnesium rather than iron.

THE HUNZA LESSON

that the fields are flooded each year by waters from mountain snows which carry the same kind of life-giving silt that nourishes the farms of Hunza. Every year thousands of tons of fresh, green grass are plowed back into the soil. Other natural compost is added to replace the grasses which have been harvested.

The methods of agriculture on this farm are similar to those of Hunza. Hence its name. Basically, the only difference is that nature deposits millions of pounds of glacial mineral ions on this farm each year, while the Hunzukuts build retaining basins to settle out these minerals. The agricultural creeds are the same:

1. That the soil is a living, breathing organism. From it comes all life's sustenance. The soil must be fed in the way of nature, the same as any animal that eats therefrom, if it is to maintain balance.

2. That glacial minerals must be added fresh to the soil each year. That is the big difference in their agricultural method and the so-called compost farmer of today. The compost is good, but it is

only half of the picture. Where are the mineral salts coming from? Not from the addition of a few trace minerals! A million dollars worth of trace minerals are deposited on this Hunza Farm each year from flood waters originating in the mineral-rich mountain rocks.

Not long after I had read the article about the Hunza Farm grass, a visitor in my office told me that he had had first-hand experience with the grass. For a period of some time, he had daily eaten the grass in a form suitable for human consumption. He believed that it provided beneficial bulk, comparable to the cellulose used in Dr. Lane's experiments as described previously.

To verify this claim about his good health in order further to substantiate my artery-to-vein ratio theory, I asked permission to examine his eyes. He readily agreed. His "ratio" was perfect—1:1.

It is true that before I went to Hunza I might have been reluctant to admit that proper nourishment and effective elimination of body wastes could

THE HUNZA LESSON

so dramatically affect a person's health and his outlook on life. However, the Hunzukuts offered proof that cannot be denied.

CHAPTER EIGHT

THE INSPIRATION OF HUNZA

GEORGE BERNARD SHAW said: "Youth is wasted on the young." It seems we have no time to enjoy life while we are young. Years go by fast, filled with studies, worries and problems, and before we are aware of it the calendar years have mounted up. Today the average American between forty and fifty is dreading the approach of old age.

Men and women alike are trying to conceal gray hair by covering it with a dye! Wrinkles and sagging lines are covered with a thick layer of makeup that only gives the face a strange look and doesn't help at all. The figure is pulled into a tight girdle in an attempt to conceal unwanted pounds, but this also doesn't help the appearance or the morale. Millions of dollars are spent in an effort to retain the effect of youth and beauty. However, the look of anxiety on the face cannot be erased by artificial means. Even a healthy person can imagine himself sick. The appearance of old age creeps in as an unwanted visitor, bringing unhappiness and a negative approach to life.

The Hunza people became a legendary saga, a mystery to the rest of the world, because they mastered the secret of old age. They live long and remain youthful in mind and body until they die. There are some people who live to be ninety or one hundred in our country, too, but they are in such minority that few know about them.

"How old are you?" seems to be such an important subject. Nevertheless we are beginning to realize that the secret of youthfulness is in our own keeping. No person who has imagination needs ever grow old, for he carries within himself the long-looked-for Fountain of Youth that Ponce de Leon sought so hopefully.

Life is a matter of going forward. Those who

THE INSPIRATION OF HUNZA

keep pace with it cannot grow old. The calendar years are not important, but a state of mind is. A mind kept vital by a spirit of enthusiasm and desire for new adventure has found the secret of eternal youth. Youth is an expression of life, and life is eternal.

Why grow old? Life is only beginning at forty. Since the world has progressed in so many things there is so much to learn it requires times to get ready for it. At forty, one should have gained enough knowledge to understand the purpose of life. Scientists are beginning to be aware that life is an endless process of growth. Our body cells are continually being renewed. The process of growth —the casting off of worn-out cells and building of new ones—continuously renews the body. Why then should cells be replaced by old or deficient ones?

We are a composite of the physical, mental and spiritual. It is up to us to unite the body, mind and spirit in complete harmony to create balance within. Life is a perpetual process of tearing down and building up. It has perfect balance, but human ignorance and error have interfered with its rhythmic equilibrium.

"You are what you eat." Food is the source of energy, and the quality of your blood depends on your diet. Natural balanced food will nourish your blood and cells and keep them vital and young—and in a healthy body there is nearly always a healthy mind, and vice versa.

In *Walden* Thoreau says: "Every man is the builder of a temple called his body, to the God he worships, after a style purely his own, nor can he get off by hammering marble instead. We are all sculptors and painters, and our material is our own flesh and blood and bone. Any nobleness begins at once to refine a man's features, any meanness or sensuality to imbrute them."

Whatever attitude we take is ours because we have made a choice. Whether we live in the mood of fear or in the mood of courage, the choice is ours. We can fix our minds on various disappointments of the day and develop a mood of resentment. Nourishing resentment will eventually sink into anger, worry and physical discomfort, which will cause anxiety and sleepless nights, leaving us not too well fitted to meet our daily responsibilities.

We are what we think we are! This is undoubtedly man's most important law of life and our well-being is in direct proportion to our understanding of this principle.

Science has proved that thoughts are powerful forces which can either build us up or tear us down. Through the unconscious or creative mind, our ways of thinking influence our nervous system and more importantly our glandular apparatus, thus regulating body chemistry. Negative or destructive thoughts can in a matter of seconds paralyze the entire network of our defense mechanisms, subjecting our body organs to stagnation and decay.

In contrast to the incredible damage that negative thoughts can do our bodies, we can bring harmony and integration to organs and functions by optimistic or constructive thoughts. All of us possess this creative capacity to think constructive or destructive thoughts. The conscious mind or will dominates the unconscious or inner force and can make it follow any desired pattern.

"What I can do, you can do also," is the secret of Christ's enlightening statement. And didn't He say, "You are made in His image"?

Doesn't this mean that we are a part of the immense universal force and are entitled to enjoy all worth-while things on earth? However, we must be sure what constitutes "worth-while" things. Does this mean the acquisition of pretentious homes, the possession of earthly wealth and power? Not exactly. Earthly riches alone without the integration of constructive thoughts will not only deprive us of internal happiness but will actually destroy our very existence, beginning at the physical level. Instead of our owning things, things will catch up with us and own us.

By now we should realize that only through ignorance and wrong thinking we get sick, grow old, deteriorate, because we believe we must. What the mind imagines, the body expresses. If the mind is kept fresh and alert, ready to accept changing conditions adaptable to new experiences, its owner has found the secret to mental stability, as well as physical well-being. It is our duty to provide a way to the truth of life, because our body responds accurately to it. After all, why should we doubt that the power which created man is not able to recreate him?

A body doesn't wear out and fall into decay because of its age, nor do its various organs waste away in the manner that constant use wears out mechanical parts. On the contrary, unused muscles become flabby and often waste away altogether; therefore, exercise is a definite source of vibrant health.

Breathing is another foundation in the structure of well-being. Breathing brings life-giving oxygen to your corpuscles and it is a source of additional vitality. There is nothing like a full breath taken at the right moment to snap tension or to banish fatigue.

Keeping the mind and body youthful is not simple. We allow the mind to grow tired and the body lazy, and fall into the rut of habit. When we are afraid to accept changes, the spirit of adventure is gone. As soon as we grow tired of life, the body will let down. The converse is also true. Those who desire eternal youth and peace of mind must cultivate an eagerness for new knowledge and experience, ignore pettiness, remain always calm and undisturbed, learn to relax, live, think and practice health, believe in good thoughts and exercise good thoughts.

It is up to us to face things as they are; to decide whether we will accept them with courage and faith or in a mood of despair. As life progresses there is a need for us all to change our ideas, our methods of doing things, our very way of living—not only our eating habits but also our thinking. Let's try to show an unyielding faith in God, in omnipresent good. Let's keep on believing that there is yet much in the world that is of great value and importance. It is not easy, but we are blessed with a Divine Power within us. If we become aware of this power we shall find it is great enough to build a new and beautiful world for us.

The people of America are known for their stability and courage. As a nation we are respected and honored for our power. Let's welcome what is good in a new idea or method. Let's try to live today the best life that we can imagine within our power to create.

It is so easy to drift along in habits that have long been established, but if we have faith in our ability to change and to grow with this change we shall earn a fuller life and know a greater peace of mind.

"The Hunzas' physical health, I believe, is an expression of their spiritual development, so beautifully shown in their love for each other and their adherence to the Golden Rule. These people know little of religious dogma yet, strange as it seems, if there is such a place as the Garden of Eden it must certainly be this enchanted valley. Can it be some instinct or intuition that enables them to know what is right from wrong; that keeps them free and orderly without policemen or jails?"*

There can be no more desirable time than now to try to build up new habits and take a constructive

* "The Dynamics of Vibrant Health," by Dr. Maxwell O. Gorten, published by the author.

attitude toward your health, your thoughts, your affairs. Accept this challenge as joy and have no fear. Remember, you have the power and privilege of choice. It is up to you alone to realize what you want in your life. Shakespeare said "Assume a virtue though you have it not." We must act the part of that which we want to be or do.

"Divine expectancy is the wind that fills the sails in the ship that is coming to you," bringing you everything you can ask for . . . health, happiness and prosperity.

> You can triumph and come to skill,
>   You can be great if you only will.
> You're well equipped for what fight you
>   choose;
>   You have arms and legs and a brain to use,
> And the man who has risen great deeds to do
>   Began his life with no more than you.
>
> *You* are the handicap you must face.
> You are the one who must choose your place.
>   You must say where you want to go,
> How much you will study the truth to know;
>   God has equipped you for life, but He
> Lets you decide what you want to be.

THE INSPIRATION OF HUNZA

Courage must come from the soul within
   The man must furnish the will to win.
So figure it out for yourself, my lad,
    You were born with all that the great
      have had,
With your equipment they all began,
    Get hold of yourself and say: "I can."

—ANONYMOUS

APPENDIX

QUESTIONS AND ANSWERS

THE information I gave on the *People Are Funny* show following my return from Hunza stimulated the interest of many of the millions of people who follow Art Linkletter's popular program. Letters came to me from all sections of the United States with pertinent questions, not only about Hunza but also regarding the food habits and health conditions in our own country.

Apparently the general public is deeply concerned about nutritional deficiencies in our diets. I am including some of the questions, with my answers, in this book with the hope that they will be of interest and assistance to my readers.

HUNZA LAND

QUESTIONS AND ANSWERS

Q. How do the Hunzukuts prevent disease from entering their country?

A. Disease cannot be prevented from entering any country. However, healthy humans, animals and plants can successfully repel disease. Witness the freedom from insects and plant disease enjoyed in Hunza agriculture.

Q. Why do not plagues destroy the people of Hunza?

A. Plagues are the result of a mass deficiency of a certain element, or group of elements, needed in human or animal bodies. The people of Hunza have never had this lack; hence, no plagues.

Q. When Hunzukuts leave their country, do they become diseased?

A. As they enter civilization and partake of foreign foods with various deficiencies, they become susceptible to the diseases of the country in which they live. If they return to Hunza before their constitutions or organs are irreparably affected, they regain their health when the Hunza diet has had time to restore their resistance.

APPENDIX

Q. How old is the oldest person in Hunza?

A. There are many, many "elders" in Hunza, and they are regarded with respect because of their age and the wisdom fostered by experience. I would say the oldest man is 120, although it is said that some have lived to 140 years.

Q. If Hunza is disease free, how does death come?

A. Like the "one hoss shay," all the Hunzukuts' bodily organs seem to expire at one time. One day the oldster is there; the next day he is gone.

Q. What do the people eat as a rule?

A. The Hunzukuts eat millet, wheat, buckwheat and barley; vegetables such as turnips, carrots, potatoes, tomatoes, corn, peas, beans and leafy vegetables; some meat (generally mutton) and milk products.

Q. What milk products do they eat?

A. Sweet milk, sour milk, butter and cheese. Goats and sheep supply most of the milk. All nutrients are preserved because pasteurization is unknown in Hunza.

HUNZA LAND

Q. Do the Hunzukuts eat eggs?

A. They import such eggs as are eaten. Because of the cost, eggs are not commonly eaten by the average native.

Q. What animals do they have?

A. Small ponies, burros and yaks are the beasts of burden in Hunza. Sheep, goats and a limited number of cattle are grown for supplying milk and its by-products. These latter animals are used for meat when their productive capacity wanes.

Q. Do Hunza animals have diseases?

A. No. Indeed, as an experiment to demonstrate disease resistance, scientists imported cattle suffering from "hoof and mouth" disease. Even though in contact with these infected animals, the local cattle did not develop this highly infectious disease. Although Hunza cattle are underfed, due to lack of forage, the food they do eat is insect-repellent, and the animals' bodies apparently repel disease in like manner.

APPENDIX

Q. Do Hunza women outlive their men as is customary in other countries?

A. The contrary is true in Hunza. Men outlive the women by an average of about five years.

Q. How large are their families?

A. As arable land, and consequent food production, is limited in Hunza, families are kept small; usually one or two children.

Q. Do the women work in the fields with the men?

A. Yes. The Hunzukuts' work day—in planting, growing and harvesting seasons—begins shortly after sun-up and lasts until the sun is setting. Thus, a minimum time is spent in the home; the "little woman" is not concerned with TV soap operas and bridge clubs. (And, there are no fat women in Hunza!)

Q. What is the customary marriage age in Hunza?

A. Eighteen is the average marriage age.

Q. Do the men have more than one wife?

A. Hunzukuts are monogamists.

HUNZA LAND

Q. Do they have divorces?

A. The Hunzukuts have tranquil dispositions, and from early childhood they are taught how to get along with others. Divorce is rare.

Q. Do they have family troubles?

A. No people on earth are free from differences—from family groups to nations, and the Hunzukuts are no exception. However, I am told, marital problems are seldom serious.

Q. How do Hunza women dress?

A. Costumes of native women are somewhat like those worn by gypsies. They are gaudy with color, and the flared skirts offer a quaint touch that is charming. Fabrics, for the most part, are home-woven from the wool of the sheep and from the hair of the ibex, yak and goat.

Q. When do they menopause?

A. Usually at the age of fifty. They reputedly suffer no menstrual pain or childbirth pain.

APPENDIX

Q. If men become fathers at ninety, what about their women?

A. It is not uncommon for men of ninety to father children in Hunza. These men, of course, have lost their first wives and have married much younger women.

Q. Do they make their own clothes?

A. Most of the Hunzukuts' clothes are homemade. Western customs, however, are seeping into Hunza, and more Western clothes are being imported.

Q. Does it rain in Hunza?

A. Yes. They have occasional flash rains, but summers are mostly arid. However, there is snow in winter, and sometimes drifts up to five feet blanket the valley. This snow augments the high-mountain snows to supply valuable water for irrigation.

Q. Does their water have any minerals in it?

A. Hunza water comes from mountain streams fed by melting ice and snow high in the mountains.

Passing over and through rocks and soil, the water picks up valuable minerals which are deposited as silt on the fields during irrigation periods. The water is dark gray in color, and the natives prefer this "dark water" for drinking purposes. Foreigners generally drink water that has been allowed to settle, and therefore is clear. I adopted the native custom and found the water very palatable.

Q. Do they employ commercial fertilizers and insecticides?

A. Commercial fertilizers are forbidden by law. The fertility of the soil is superior because only natural elements are used to enrich it. Everything that is taken from the soil is returned to the soil. As pests are negligible, insecticides are unnecessary.

Q. Do the people of Hunza have good teeth? Do they use toothbrushes or dentifrices?

A. They have very good teeth. Although they have no toothbrushes or dentifrices, they clean their teeth and stimulate their gums by the use of small twigs.

APPENDIX

Q. Is Hunza part of another country?

A. Hunza chose to become a part of Pakistan. It is governed by special laws devised for frontier states, such as Swat, Dir and Chitral (they have their own rulers). Pakistan does not interfere in the internal affairs of Hunza. The Mir holds the title of "Honorable Rank of Brigadier" in the Pakistan army.

Q. How did the Mir get his kingdom?

A. From ancient days, rulership has been handed down from father to eldest son. The second son then becomes the servant of the new Mir; he never marries and remains the constant companion and assistant of the Mir.

Q. What are the names of the royal family?

A. Muhammad O. H. D. Jamal Khan, Ruler of Hunza State: Honorable Rank of Brigadier in the Pakistan Army; Ghazi Milat and Hilali, Pakistan. "Mir" means ruler, which precedes his name.

Her Highness, Rani, of Hunza, Queen of Hunza.

Prince Ayash Khan (brother of the Mir).

HUNZA LAND

Prince Ghazanfar Ali Khan (Crown Prince)
Princess Duri Shahwar (Eldest married daughter of the Mir).
Prince Amen Khan (Second Prince).
Prince Abbas Khan (Third Prince).
Princess Nilofar (Second Princess).
Princess Malika Hussn (Third Princess).
Princess Mehr Ul Jamal, also called Merry (Fourth Princess).
Princess Fauzia (Fifth Princess).
Princess Azra (Sixth Princess).
The children of the Royal Family were tutored by an American and his wife, Mr. and Mrs. Win Mumby, for the past five years. All the children speak and write English.

Q. Is the Mir of Hunza friendly to America?

A. Yes, most friendly. His Highness is extremely anxious to visit this country, and he particularly wants to see New York City, Washington, D.C., and Hollywood. Undoubtedly, he will appear on television, and he will prove a genuinely interesting attraction because he is fluent and witty and speaks excellent English.

APPENDIX

Q. Do they have money? How much do they spend?

A. Hunza does not have a national currency. They use Pakistanian money, which is roughly five rupees to the United States dollar. However, the people have very little money, and they transact such business as they do mostly by barter. The curse of inflation has not overlooked even this small country.

Q. Can we import food from Hunza?

A. No. Hunza does not have sufficient food to permit export; and United States customs and agricultural laws would prevent it. There is no canning (or preserving) of fruits and vegetables in Hunza, and even many of our states have laws prohibiting passage of unprocessed produce across their borders.

Q. Could I cure a disease by going to Hunza?

A. If none of your vital organs is functionally destroyed, recovery may be possible. Many Hunzukuts go to Pakistan to live, and some of them "return home to die." Many of those who return live several more years of happy, active life.

HUNZA LAND

Q. Do people in Hunza have vitamins?

A. Commercial vitamins are unknown in Hunza, and they are not needed. All the nutrients necessary to health are supplied by the Hunza soil which is nourished naturally.

Q. What is the difference between natural and synthetic vitamins?

A. Natural vitamins are taken from natural sources —from insect-repellent produce raised in naturally enriched soil. They contain important trace elements. Synthetic vitamins are manufactured from coal tar and other substances and they contain no trace elements.

Q. Are health food stores any good?

A. Yes, they are invaluable sources for the natural foods we need to build our bodies and keep them in radiant good health. These stores offer countless life-giving foods that cannot be obtained elsewhere.

Q. I have been taking vitamins and have not been feeling any better. Do I need them?

APPENDIX

A. Yes, if you live in the United States. Our soil is far too depleted and our foods too highly processed to provide the nourishment healthy bodies need. However, the type of vitamins you take is important. Even though potencies may be the same, natural vitamins are superior to synthetic. Besides, natural vitamins contain trace elements not found in the other type.

Q. We have an organic wheat field and stone grind our wheat for bread. How do we know the soil is suitable for vegetables?

A. If you plant vegetables in that field and they repel insects, the soil is suitable. If they do not repel insects, additional natural fertilizer will be needed to supply missing elements. Insects are the index as to whether a soil is proper for a healthy plant.

Q. How do we make compost? Is it possible for farmers to have enough for their fields?

A. Several natural-farming books and magazines are available. Information can be obtained from Organic Gardening and Farming, 46 South West Street, Allentown, Pennsylvania. Natural compost can be manufactured at prices comparable to those of commercial fertilizer. Plants are now in operation in many places, and a new plant will be located in Kearney, Nebraska.

Q. Do you know whether or not there is soil similar to Hunza's in the United States?

A. There is a farm at the foot of the mountains near Duvall, Washington, which has a soil very much like that of Hunza. The waters from the mountains bring down mineral-rich silt which is a major factor in producing plants of truly amazing nutritive value.

Q. Are the people of Hunza intelligent?

A. The Hunzukuts are given a high intelligence rating by Western visitors to the little country. It is surprising to find such natural intellect in a people inhabiting a part of the world noted for low mentality. Examples of Hunzukut intellect are found in their remarkably effective agriculture, their food handling methods, their ingenuity in building an irrigation system, and their non-fanatical approach to religion. The stock from which the race developed and the food they

APPENDIX

have eaten for centuries are probably responsible for the mental superiority of the Hunzukuts.

Q. Do they believe in exercise?

A. Exercise for the Hunzukuts does not depend on a belief. Their way of life demands exercise every day from dawn until dusk during the crop growing seasons. The remarkable health and stamina of the natives are undoubtedly due to the fact that exercise is a part of their life from earliest years.

Q. Does breathing mountain air have any influence on their health?

A. I believe good air and proper breathing have a great deal to do with the vitality of the Hunzukuts. Their active life and the mountainous terrain of their country force deep breathing habits upon the people of all ages. From early childhood they practice the art of breathing, inhaling the pure fresh air. Wonderfully helpful information about this subject is contained in *Yoga for Americans* and *Forever Young—Forever Healthy,* both books by Indra Devi, published by Prentice-Hall, Inc., Englewood Cliffs, New Jersey.

HUNZA LAND

Q. Are the people warlike?

A. Quite the contrary. Centuries ago they were spirited fighters because they had to defend the mountain passes against intruders. However, present-day Hunzukuts are the most even-tempered, good-natured individuals I have ever seen.

Q. Is it possible for anyone to enter Hunza?

A. Access to Hunza is becoming easier; new roads are being built which will eliminate most of the hazards of the trip. Security screening is necessary, of course, and entrance permisssion must be granted in advance by the Pakistan government. American tourists are welcome, both in Pakistan and Hunza, and both countries are friendly towards the United States. A surprising number of Americans are found in Pakistan today.

Q. Does it get cold in the winter? Do they ski?

A. It gets very cold in the winter, often fifteen or more degrees below zero. Hunza mountainsides are much too steep and rocky for skiing, and snow is unevenly distributed.

APPENDIX

Q. What are their sports?

A. Polo is the national game in Hunza—comparable to baseball in the United States. The boys start young, on foot; they graduate to small burros, horses and yaks. The game is a rough one, and rules are apparently non-existent. Missing teeth are the proud badges of the polo enthusiasts. Other strenuous contests such as running, mountain climbing, swimming, wrestling and javelin throwing are popular. Hunting is both a sport and a means of augmenting the scarce meat supply. Marco Polo sheep and ibex are choice quarry. For women, sports are confined to sewing and housekeeping.

Q. Why don't people of Hunza live forever?

A. It is not ordained that humans shall live forever. However, the Hunzukuts, a unique race, enjoy a much longer life and a healthier one than is customary. In my opinion, the Hunzukuts would live even longer if they had more land and more natural fertilizer. At present, the country is overpopulated, and it is necessary to import food. The population is now over 25,000; fifty years

HUNZA LAND

ago it was 7,000. The amount of arable land remains the same. Diseases will result from eating deficient foods, and the life span of people will inevitably be shortened. Probably Hunza will go the way of all civilizations.

Q. Do the men of Hunza smoke?

A. I would say that about two per cent of the men smoke. According to latest research, natural vitamin C should be added to the daily diet by all users of tobacco.

Q. Do you recommend whole grain cereals?

A. Whole grains are essential in the planning of healthful, vital meals. Children need the minerals in whole grains to meet the body requirements; adults for body repair. Only by eating 100 per cent whole wheat bread or other whole grain products do we get the full benefit of the important nutrients which nature has put into whole grains.

Q. What does modern milling do to whole wheat?

A. Modern milling reduces both the quantity and

APPENDIX

quality of the proteins. One half of the fat and a great number of vitamins and minerals, which are nutritionally very important, are lost in milling.

CPSIA information can be obtained
at www.ICGtesting.com
Printed in the USA
LVHW081358250719
625335LV00025B/381/P